The ...de to

D...ve

Ne...ts

KT-513-861

The Beginner's Guide to Decorative Needlecrafts

Embroidery • Cross Stitch • Beading • Quilting and Appliqué

Charlotte Gerlings

ARCTURUS

ARCTURUS

This edition published in 2014 by Arcturus Publishing Limited
26/27 Bickels Yard, 151–153 Bermondsey Street,
London SE1 3HA

ISBN: 978-1-78212-967-7
AD004095UK

Illustrated by David Woodroffe
With special thanks to Diana Vowles

p8: Materials provided and photographed by kind permission of DMC
Creative World Ltd (visit www.dmccreative.co.uk to find out more), and
Madeira UK (www.madeira.co.uk)

Printed in China

INTRODUCTION

After mastering the basics of sewing, people often like to try more elaborate or challenging techniques but are not sure where to start. *The Beginner's Guide to Decorative Needlecrafts* presents a package of mini-tutorials on four decorative needlecrafts: Embroidery; Quilting and Appliqué; Beadweaving; and Cross Stitch, any one of which will help you gain expertise and inspire your creativity.

The decorative crafts in this book vary in terms of materials and methods. It is quite likely that you will be able to experiment with things you already have around the house. Then comes the time when you wish to progress with a particular craft and this guide contains lists of equipment you will need, together with instructions on how to use the less familiar items among them.

The guide also includes the use of a sewing machine and features illustrated advice for first-time users as well as for those wanting to update the skills they learned in the past. The sections contain information on specific materials and quantities required; tips on creating and interpreting patterns; glossaries of terms; and a number of simple projects to develop your abilities and increase your confidence.

Applying decoration to work, domestic and personal objects is second nature to human beings everywhere, and decorative needlecrafts have always made a delightful contribution to household linens, soft furnishings, clothes and fashion accessories. Eventually, you may realize you have discovered a new career, or you may simply have developed an addiction to decorative needlecrafts for pleasure. Whichever is the case, the journey will be a fascinating one.

CONTENTS

BEADWEAVING

CROSS STITCH

THREADS

1 Aida (block weave) fabric   2 Evenweave fabric   3 Perle [pearl] cotton twist   4 6-stranded polyester
5 6-stranded rayon   6 6-stranded cotton   7 Blending filament   8 Metallic hand- or machine embroidery thread
9 Metallic twist for embroidery, tassels and cords (divisible)   10 6-stranded metallic polyester
11 Matt soft cotton (stranded)   12 Perle [pearl] cotton twist, plain and variegated

EMBROIDERY

Different writers have attempted to define 'embroidery'. Most commonly, it is described as 'thread worked on an existing fabric by hand or machine'. Sometimes embroidery is referred to as 'needlework' or the embellishment of fabric, enriching it with needle and thread.

Hand stitches have been around for as long as there have been needles, and hand embroidery for as long as people wanted to decorate woven fabric, felt or leather. Embroidery stitches come from very different origins. Some undoubtedly have their foundation in early textiles, basketry, mat-making and weaving; others have developed from early sewing. It is not surprising then, that there is a wide range of names for them and this can cause confusion.

Stitches are produced by needle and thread being inserted and brought out through the fabric at specific intervals. This action, the repetition of actions, and grouping of threads, produces an endless variety of surfaces and combinations of effects. Today, embroidery can be used in many ways and for outcomes that are practical or ornamental, as well as those that express a concept and have no practical application.

Like workers in other arts and crafts you have to make a start somewhere and I am sure that once you allow the stitches to be used in a way that pleases you, you will be bitten by the bug and want to continue learning and expressing ideas, patterns, whatever, using the marks that embroidery stitches can make.

You don't have to know or use a large number of stitches to make embroidery. However, you do need a needle, thread and fabric that are sympathetic, one to the other. There is nothing more frustrating than tugging your thread through a fabric because you have the wrong materials. Get that right before you start. Stitch away from or towards yourself – people do stitch in different directions, left- or right-handed – you will discover what is most comfortable for you.

Be patient and true to what you like. It's fine to make large rough stitches or small precious ones, there is no right or wrong way to use them – but you may have to practise with different fabrics and threads to achieve the desired effect.

If you have no idea where to start then perhaps you could look at Indian embroidery. Some of the most wonderful embroidery is still made in India and you can find many examples in our shops and museum collections.

Anne Morrell

Professor Anne Morrell was formerly principal lecturer at Manchester Metropolitan University Department of Textiles/Fashion, which has the only embroidery degree course in the UK. She is currently consultant to the Ahmedabad Calico Museum in Gujarat, India, where she visits each year, systematically recording and documenting traditional Indian textile techniques.

PART ONE:
EQUIPMENT AND MATERIALS

NEEDLES

Needles are manufactured in a wide range of lengths and thicknesses; the higher the number, the finer the needle. Take care to select the right size and type of needle for the thread and fabric you are using.

1 **Sharps** Medium-length and pointed, with a round eye, for general sewing with cotton or polyester thread.

2 **Crewel or embroidery** Pointed like sharps but with a long oval eye like a tapestry needle, for thicker or multiple threads.

3 **Tapestry** Blunt-tipped with a long oval eye, used in counted thread embroidery.

4 **Betweens** Short and sharp, with a small round eye. Used for fine stitching and quilting.

5 **Milliner's or straws** Very long and thin with a round eye, used for applying decoration.

6 **Bodkin** Thick, blunt-tipped, with an eye large enough to carry cord, elastic or ribbon through loops and casings.

7 **Glover's or leather** Has a sharp 3-sided tip for piercing leather and PVC without tearing.

Needle eyes

Needle eyes are either round or oval; round ones are the smallest and long oval the largest. Although a small needle helps with fine work, if the eye is too tight around the thread or yarn, it will be difficult to pull through the fabric and could fray the thread in the process.

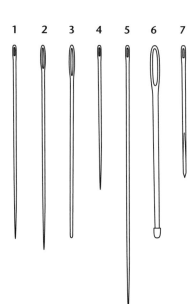

Most needles are nickel plated, though the quality varies. They sometimes become discoloured and may mark your work if left in the fabric; put them away when you have finished. Some people keep a tiny cushion packed firmly with emery powder, which is a useful abrasive for cleaning needles and pins. Gold- and platinum-plated needles will not discolour or rust but are more expensive.

THREADS

Embroidery threads can be bought in balls, on spools, or in skeins and hanks (see the selection on the rear cover and key information on p. 2). The shawl border below was worked in silver and gold but there is no reason why embroiderers shouldn't try anything from ribbon to string or fine wire.

Choose threads in natural light if possible because artificial lighting intensifies certain colours and dulls others. The fibres that you choose are important for the texture or finish of your embroidery and always bear in mind the end use of whatever you make. Do not buy cheap machine thread – it breaks easily and may not perform very smoothly. It could also shrink or run in the wash.

Stranded cotton [floss] Often called 'silk' and the most commonly used embroidery thread. It consists of six divisible strands and is packaged in a small skein.

Perle [pearl] cotton Shiny 2-ply twisted thread. Unlike stranded cotton, it cannot be separated into strands. However, it is available in various thicknesses.

Soft cotton Thick, stranded cotton, unmercerized, with a matt finish. Ideal for novices working on the 6-count (six holes per inch) block-weave fabric known as 'Binca'.

Stranded rayon High-gloss six-stranded thread [floss].

Z-twist rayon Glossy 4-ply twist, spun clockwise.

Metallic threads A wide category; metallics are slightly abrasive with a tendency to fray at the ends. Use a large-eyed needle to make a bigger hole in the cloth and reduce the drag on both thread and fabric. For this reason it is best to work with short lengths.

Blending filament Very fine metallic thread for blending with others in the same needle, to create special effects (p. 19).

Space-dyed (or variegated) threads Factory-dyed in multiple colours, or in shades of a single colour, at regular intervals along the thread.

Hand-dyed threads Dyed by hand using one or more colours, possibly neither light- nor colour-fast.

Machine embroidery threads Available in plain and variegated colours like those for hand embroidery. Most threads are numbered from 100 to 12, where the larger number means a finer thread. If using a digitized embroidery pattern, load up with a size 40 thread. Those thicker than size 30 are generally too heavy for most embroidery designs. Shiny machine threads add lustre to close stitching such as satin stitch. Their softness and pliability work well for free-motion stitching.

Cotton machine embroidery thread Usually size 50 but the matt finish gives it a thicker appearance.

Polyester machine embroidery thread Colourfast and durable. Compatible with rayon so they may be run together.

Rayon machine embroidery thread Tends to slip so it is advisable to wind the bobbin with matching cotton or polyester thread and keep the shiny rayon for the top surface of your piece. Rayon dyes can fade with strong sunlight or frequent washing.

Silk Obtainable on spools for machine sewing. Check whether it is washable or dry-clean only.

You can buy shade cards, including actual thread samples, from major manufacturers such as DMC, Anchor, Coats, Madeira and Kreinik and they are obtainable from online needlecraft suppliers. Software is also available to provide accurate colour matching across the different thread brands.

FABRIC

The background texture and colour of your fabric is important. Modern fabrics consist of natural or man-made fibres, often mixed to combine their best qualities.

Crewel cockatrice

Crewel embroidery was traditionally worked in wool on linen twill fabric. This 17th century cockatrice would have formed part of the densely stitched decoration for some elaborate bed hangings. Twill is substantial and makes a fine, long-lasting upholstery fabric.

Woven fabric

Every woven fabric belongs to one of three types:

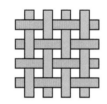

Plain weave Alternate warp (lengthwise) threads go over one and under one of the weft (crosswise) threads. Linen, poplin, muslin and organza are familiar examples.

Twill weave Interlaces warp and weft threads over and under two or more threads progressively, to produce a clear diagonal pattern on hardwearing fabrics like denim or gabardine.

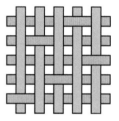

Satin weave A smooth, glossy, compact surface created by long silky 'floats' that leave no weft visible; the reverse is matt.

The grain

The grain of a fabric is the direction in which the warp and weft threads lie. The warp runs lengthwise, parallel to the selvedge [selvage]: this is the *lengthwise grain*. The weft follows the *crosswise grain*, at right angles to the selvedge [selvage].

Selvedge [selvage]

Lengthwise grain
Warp threads

Crosswise grain
Weft threads

Bias

The bias

The bias lies along any diagonal line between the lengthwise and crosswise grains. True bias is at the 45-degree angle where you will get the maximum stretch. Bias strips are often used for piping and binding edges because of their flexibility on curves and corners.

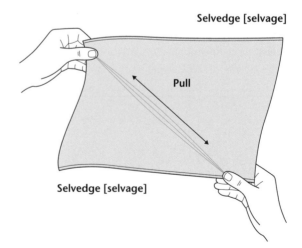

Selvedge [selvage]

Pull

Selvedge [selvage]

Counted thread fabrics

The two most widely used fabrics for counted cross stitch come in a range of neutral tones and colours.

Aida

This block weave fabric is favoured by beginners because of its regular construction and visible stitch holes. It also has a stiffer finish for hand-held work. It is worth noting that unworked areas have a very distinct texture compared with evenweave, so be sure this is the effect you want.

Evenweave and aida are interchangeable with the aid of a little arithmetic. So, if a pattern calls for 28-count evenweave stitched over 2 threads of the fabric, use a 14-count aida and stitch into every hole instead. In the same way, you would replace 32-count evenweave with 16-count aida, and 22-count with 11-count.

Evenweave

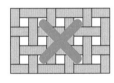

An evenweave is any natural or man-made fabric having the same number of threads per inch (2.5 cm) counted vertically and horizontally; this keeps the Cross stitches square and even.
It is frequently made of either linen or cotton.

Evenweave threads are usually of uniform thickness, though the pure linens are slightly less regular. Cross stitch is worked over two threads, so you will stitch into alternate holes. The greater the thread count per inch, sometimes given as HPI (holes per inch), the finer the cloth and the smaller your stitches will be.

Luxury fabrics

The sumptuous clothing of the Byzantines (395–1453 CE) frequently employed the art of the embroiderer. They were especially fond of geometric patterns, also flowers and leaves, often incorporating birds or mythological creatures. Many types of thread were used, including gold, and silk in vivid reds, blues, purples and yellows.

The Byzantine influence extended west and north throughout the Middle Ages (c. 500–c. 1500 CE). The highly prized medieval English embroidery called Opus Angelicanum was worked in gold thread on velvet or silk twill, and traded all across Europe. It was acquired by royalty, and by the Church for ecclesiastical vestments.

The tighter the weave, the less likely a fabric is to shrink during or after manufacture. The shop label will say if a fabric is pre-shrunk. If not, and if necessary, shrink it yourself before use. Wash and dry according to the care label, which will also reveal whether the fabric is colourfast.

BASIC EQUIPMENT

A   Needles, pins and
    pincushion

B   Thimble

C   Seam ripper

D   Dressmaking shears

E   Scissors

F   Embroidery scissors

G   Iron

H   Sewing machine

I   Embroidery threads

J   **Laying tool:** a small pointed
    stick of metal or wood for
    smoothing and straightening
    embroidery threads as you
    stitch (a yarn darner will do
    as well)

K   Masking tape

L   Embroiderers' transfer
    pencil

M   Fabric marking pencil

N   Magnifying lamp

O   Graph paper for charting
    designs

P   Dressmakers' carbon paper

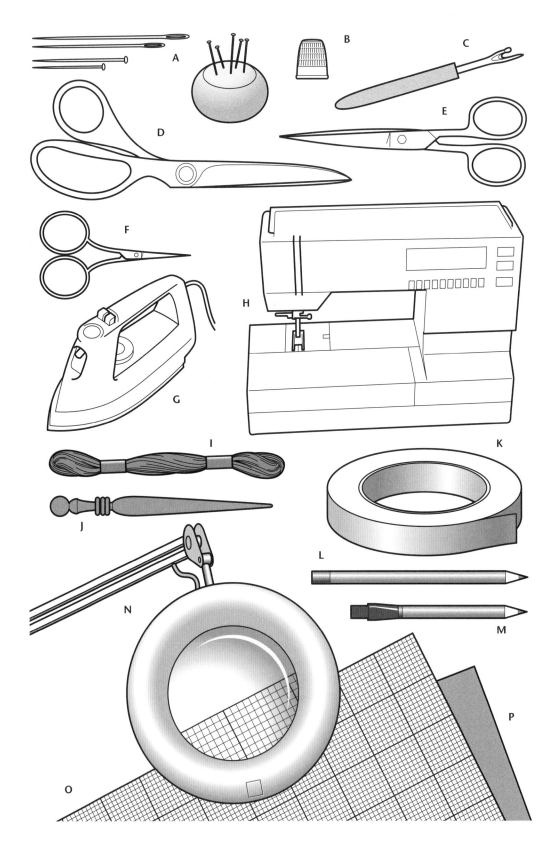

WORKING WITH HOOPS AND FRAMES

Hoops and frames are not essential equipment – many embroiderers prefer to work 'in hand' – but progress is generally quicker and more accurate when the ground fabric is evenly stretched and supported.

Hoops and frames

A standard embroidery hoop (A), also known as a tambour (pp. 46 and 51), consists of an inner and outer ring of wood or plastic. The fabric is first placed over the inner ring and the outer one is fastened around both by tightening the metal screw.

Avoid hoop marks on your fabric by first wrapping both rings with bias binding or placing tissue paper between the outer ring and the embroidery (tear the tissue away from the stitching area). Remove the hoop when you are not working.

A hoop or frame (B) of any size can be mounted on a stand (C and D) or in a clamp (E), leaving both hands free for stitching. Many people find that stabbing the needle up and down through the fabric, with one hand above and one below, is comfortable and helps to reduce any pain or cramping of the hands and wrists.

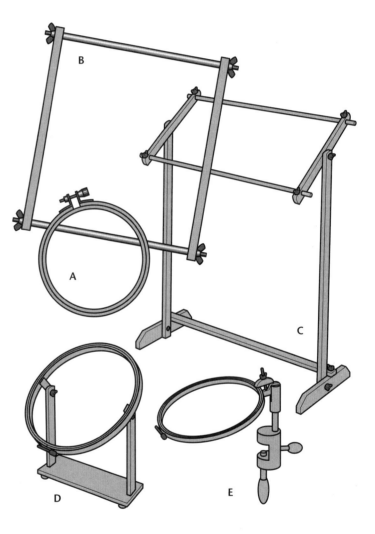

Slate frame

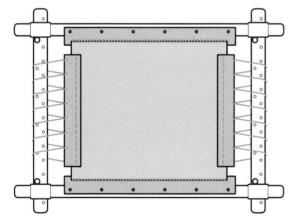

Despite its name, a 'slate' frame is made from wood. First stitch your fabric top and bottom to the strips of tape attached to the rollers. Roll any excess fabric around one roller before slotting on and pegging the two flat sides to complete the frame. Stretch the fabric tight and sew a strip of tape down both sides. With a curved needle and strong thread, lace the fabric evenly over each side of the frame, tighten, and secure firmly at the ends.

TRANSFERRING YOUR DESIGN

Here are three standard techniques for transferring a design onto fabric.

Scaling a design

(Reverse the size order below to make the image larger)

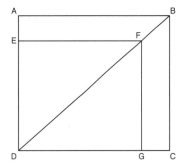

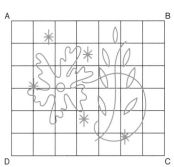

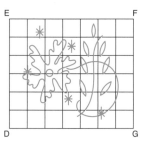

1 Trace the design and enclose in the rectangle ABCD. Draw a diagonal line from D to B. Measure and mark either the reduced height (ED) or width (DG) and with the aid of a set square, draw parallel lines across and up to the diagonal (DB), to meet at point F.

2 Divide the rectangle ABCD into squares across the original design.

3 Rule up a smaller sheet, the same size as EFGD, into the same number of divisions and copy the original, square by square until the reduced design is complete.

Tracing with carbon paper

Draw or trace a design onto thin paper. Place a sheet of dressmakers' carbon paper face down on RS of fabric (use a light colour for dark fabric and vice versa). Place design on top, and pin all three together. Draw firmly over design once more to transfer image onto fabric.

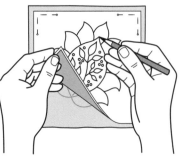

Hot-iron transfer

Draw a design on tracing paper. Turn it over and trace reversed image with an embroiderers' transfer pencil. With transfer side down, pin paper to RS of fabric. Press down directly onto paper with low-heat iron for a few seconds. Do not drag or image may smudge.

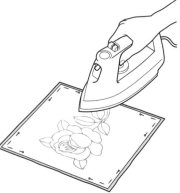

PREPARING FABRIC

Almost any fabric can be embroidered, from finest silk organza to felt or leather. Whether working in the hand or on a frame, the fabric has first to be prepared; for example, by pressing out creases, cutting away the selvedge [selvage], or maybe dyeing or colour spraying.

Sometimes the ground fabric is used alone, and sometimes a backing of mull (stiff muslin) or fine cotton is tacked [basted] on for strength. A very small or irregular shape can be tacked on to a larger piece for ease of working. Cut a hole into the supporting fabric on the wrong side so the embroidery is made on the top layer only. For use of stabilizers, see p. 46.

Four ways of keeping raw edges neat

With 3 and 4, be aware that you will have to cut away 1 cm [½ in] all round afterwards. Chemicals and adhesives will damage the fabric in the long run.

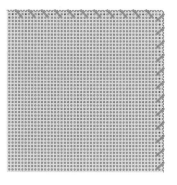

1 Overstitch around the edges by hand with sewing cotton, or roll a small hem if you wish.

2 Zigzag stitch round the edges with a sewing machine.

3 Apply an anti-fray fluid sparingly and allow to dry before working.

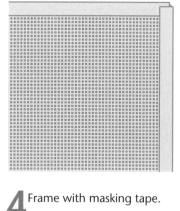

4 Frame with masking tape.

Thread organizer You might like to make an organizer for use during your project. Cut one thread of each colour to a working length (about 45 cm [18 in]) and loop it through a card with the corresponding number of holes punched down one side, where it remains ready for the needle. With project name at the top and the manufacturer's shade number beside each hole, you will also have a handy record card when finished.

Metallic threads tend to twist or break more easily, so it is advisable to cut those into shorter lengths (about 30 cm [12 in]). They also tend to unravel at the ends, which can be stopped with anti-fray fluid. Ends can be prepared in advance on the thread organizer and eventually trimmed off.

PREPARING THREADS

How many strands to use

As a rule, the number of strands of cotton [floss] that you sew with generally matches the thickness of one thread pulled out from the edge of the ground fabric.

Separating and recombining stranded cotton [floss]

Multiple strands of cotton [floss] used straight from the skein can produce bumpy stitches so it is worth taking the trouble to separate the strands, smooth them straight and put them together again in the same direction. This will reduce twisting and tangling, and the stitches will lie better.

Grip one strand firmly at the top and draw your other hand down taking the remaining threads with you until the single strand is free. The others will bunch up but won't become knotted. Finally, lay all the strands out straight and reassemble them as you wish.

Single strand outline

Many pictorial cross stitch designs are outlined in back stitch. This is often sewn in black with just one or two strands of cotton [floss].

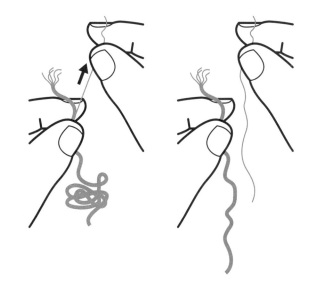

Tweeding

Different coloured strands threaded into the same needle is known as tweeding. Achieved by separating strands (see above), it is a good way of introducing textural effects and also of creating extra colours without buying more; for instance, blue and pink strands will produce mauve. There is also a very fine metallic thread known as a blending filament designed for combination with ordinary stranded cotton [floss].

The blending filament and stranded cotton [floss] will not slip when the filament is threaded up as shown. The cotton is threaded up afterwards in the usual way.

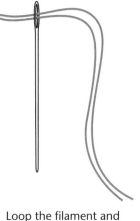

1 Loop the filament and thread it into the needle.

2 Thread the free ends through the loop.

3 Pull the ends of the filament very gently to secure it in the eye of the needle.

STARTING AND FASTENING OFF

No knots

Knots at the back will appear as unsightly bumps on the front of your work when it is finally pressed and mounted. They will even pop right through the weave if it is loose enough. So, when starting out, push your needle through from the wrong side leaving a 3 cm [1½ in] tail of thread at the back. Hold the tail against the fabric as you go and it will soon be caught down by the new stitches.

The correct way to fasten off is to run the thread under three or four wrong-side stitches, either horizontally or vertically. Whipping the end around one of those stitches helps to secure it.

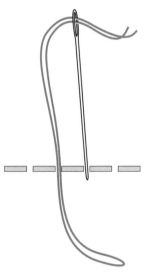

Waste knots

First knot the end of the thread and from the right side push your needle through to the back, leaving the knot on the surface of the fabric. Next, bring your needle through again about 2.5 cm [1 in] from the knot and start stitching towards it. Stab stitch steadily and be sure of completely covering the thread at the back. When that is done, trim the knot from the front.

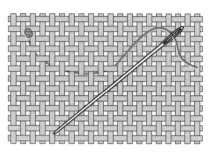

An away waste knot is placed well away from the stitching and is not covered by it. When cut off, it leaves a longer tail at the back, which is threaded into a needle and woven in.

The loop start or lark's head knot

Two conditions hold for this method: first, working with an even number of strands of cotton [floss]; and second, the working length of thread should be doubled to 90 cm [36 in].

Separate one strand of cotton [floss] if you are stitching with two strands (two for four, and three for six). Fold the strand(s) double and thread the loose ends into your needle.

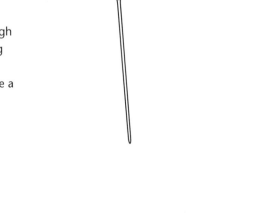

I Stab the needle up through the fabric from the wrong to the right side and pull enough thread with it to leave a small loop at the back.

2 Make your first stitch and, with the needle back on the wrong side, pass it through the waiting loop.

3 As you pull the thread it will draw the loop neatly against the fabric.

STITCH DIRECTORY

The stitches in this directory are arranged in 'families', which makes for interesting comparisons and possibilities. See p. 61 for an alphabetical list. The illustrations show when the needle actually goes in and out of the fabric and when it passes behind a part of the stitch being made without piercing the fabric.

KNOTTED STITCHES

French knot

1 Wrap thread twice around the needle and pull gently to tighten coils towards the tip.

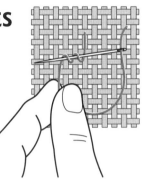 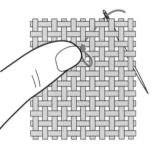

2 Insert needle, press thumb down to hold coils and pull thread gently but firmly through fabric, leaving a perfect knot on the surface.

Bullion knot

Use a straight needle with a narrow eye so thread passes as smoothly as possible through the coils. Hold coils with thumb until needle and thread are through. Turn to complete stitch and tighten carefully.

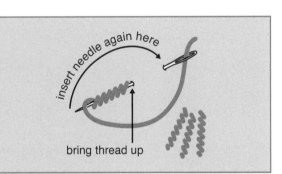

insert needle again here

bring thread up

Four-legged knot

1 Make a vertical stitch and hold thread across halfway point while sliding needle down diagonally from right to left. Thread hangs in a loop below the vertical.

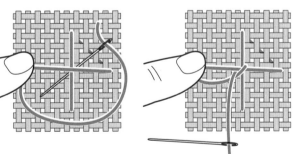

2 Pull needle and thread carefully through loop to form a knot around the centre. Take needle left, level with knot, and insert to complete cross.

Knotted stitch

Make a single diagonal stitch, perform a double loop over and insert needle immediately below. Pull through to form knot.

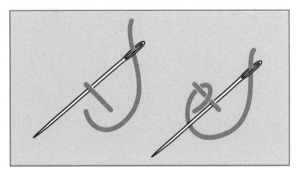

RUNNING AND BACK STITCHES

Running stitch

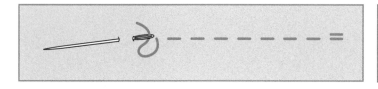

Secure thread with two small stitches. With needle at front, push into fabric and out again in one move. Stitch and space should be of equal length. Fasten off with a back stitch.

Back stitch

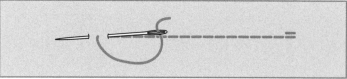

Begin exactly as for running stitch then stitch back over the first space. Needle out again at one stitch space ahead of the last stitch made. Repeat with needle back in again at the point where the previous stitch ended.

Double running (Holbein) stitch

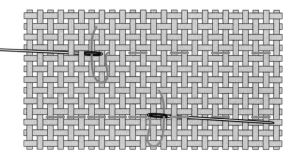

Looks like back stitch but actually consists of two passes of running stitch, where the second pass returns and precisely fills the gaps left by the first. Done with precision, this makes a far neater underside than that of back stitch. Ideal for unlined items such as bookmarks.

Double running steps

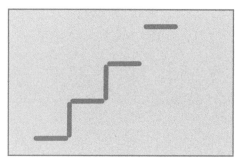

Stepped stitches constructed in two passes. Here vertical running stitches fill the gaps between the horizontal ones. Stitches must be of equal length and at perfect right angles to each another.

Dog-tooth (Bosnian) stitch

Worked in a similar way to double running. Oblique stitches return along a line of evenly spaced verticals. Also suitable for counted thread work.

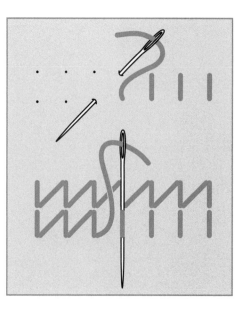

Threaded running stitch

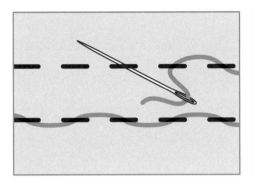

Slide the needle up and down through the line of running stitch, without piercing the fabric until the end. Finish off on the wrong side. Looks most effective when a second colour is used for the threading.

Whipped running stitch

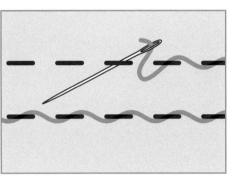

Another effective use of a second colour. Whip by sliding the needle through each running stitch in one direction only. Like threaded running, this is done without piercing the fabric until the end. Finish off on the wrong side.

Double threaded back stitch

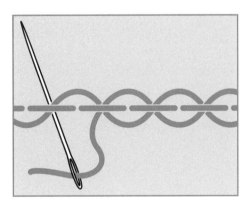

Double threading produces a heavy line. Slide the needle up and down through the stitches, without piercing the fabric until the end. Finish off on the wrong side. Repeat until the stitches are completely threaded above and below.

Pekinese stitch

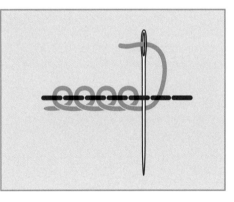

First work a line of small back stitches then loop the second thread through the stitches without piercing the fabric. The second thread travels forward two stitches and back one with each complete threading action.

Trellis back stitch

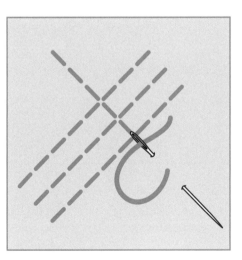

This is a diagonal arrangement of back stitched lines. The ends of the stitches should meet.

STRAIGHT AND CROSS STITCHES

Speckling

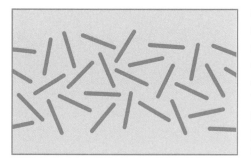

Quite small, straight stitches made in different directions and evenly distributed. This is a useful filling stitch for providing texture to a particular area.

Arrowhead stitch

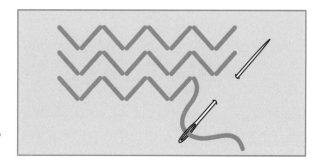

Worked vertically or horizontally, the stitches should always be at right angles to each other. Combines well with other stitches, and is also suitable for counted thread work.

Fern stitch

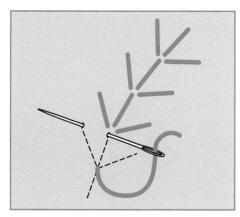

Consists of three parts, which may either be all the same length (as shown) or stitched so that the 'branches' form a leaf shape. In its linear form, Fern is a decorative means of fastening appliqué.

Fishbone stitch

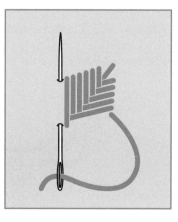

Close-woven stitches are worked from the outer edge in to a central line where they overlap.

Sheaf stitch (single)

Suitable for counted thread work. Work three straight stitches vertically or horizontally. Bring needle up halfway and pass twice around all three stitches without piercing the fabric, tighten, and insert a second time alongside the first.

Cross stitch

Cross stitch is worked by the counted thread method on an evenly woven fabric (p. 13). The most important rule about cross stitch is that all the top stitches go in one direction for a uniform appearance.

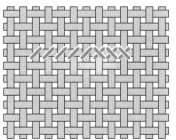

The traditional English method completes each X before moving on to the next.

The Danish method stitches one leg of the Xs first, and completes them on a return pass.

Smyrna (double cross) stitch

Using the counted thread method, one cross stitch has another cross worked vertically over it. Follow the numbered points.

Boxed cross stitch

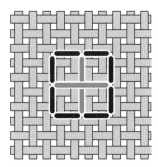

Using the counted thread method, work a vertical cross stitch. Box in with a square formation of back stitches or double running.

Woven (braided) cross

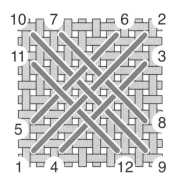

Using the counted thread method, follow the numbered points, weaving the final 3 stitches in and out of the first set.

Algerian eye stitch

1 Bring needle through at left base and work 8 straight stitches clockwise into the same central hole, following the numbered points.

2 Pull stitches firmly to create the central hole. Do not allow threads on wrong side to cover it.

Long-armed cross stitch

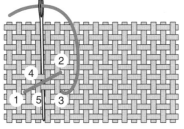

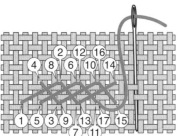

1 Following the numbers, stitch a long diagonal right. Needle in at top and out directly below. Cross over previous stitch. Needle in at top and out again below.

2 Repeat to form a row, following the numbered points. Repeated rows make a bold background filling.

Rice stitch

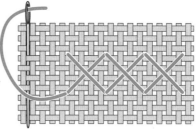

1 Work a row of counted cross stitch on an evenly woven fabric.

2 In a second colour and with finer thread, work a back stitch over each half leg of each cross stitch to form the characteristic diamond shapes.

Herringbone stitches

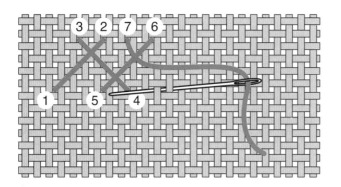

Basic herringbone stitch a long diagonal from left to right. Insert needle at top and bring out left. Crossing the previous stitch, make another diagonal right and down. Needle in at base and out left. Repeat to form a row, following the numbered points.

Threaded herringbone stitch

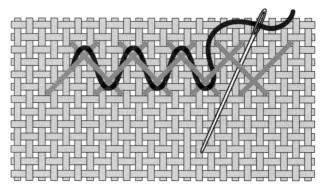

Work a row of herringbone stitch. Secure second colour thread on wrong side by whipping round existing stitches. Bring needle through and weave in and out of herringbone without piercing the fabric. Needle in and fasten off on wrong side.

Tied herringbone stitch

Work a zigzag line of coral stitch (p. 30) over a foundation of herringbone.

STEM, SPLIT, FLY AND FEATHER STITCHES

Stem stitch

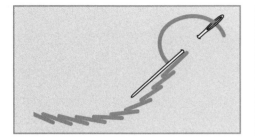

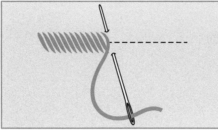

1 To follow curves or straight lines, work slanted back stitch with the needle coming out a little above the previous stitch.

2 Create a thicker, more rope-like effect by inserting the needle at a sharper angle and increasing the number of strands of thread.

Raised band stem stitch

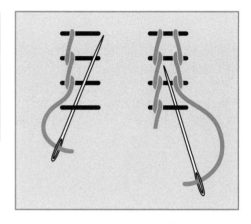

Begin working stem stitch over a series of foundation bars without piercing the fabric (left). Work symmetrically from each side inward (right). Use as a single band or as a filler.

Split stitch   ## Fly stitch

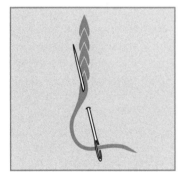

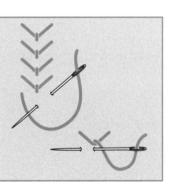

A small, delicate line stitch usually worked with silk in a frame. The needle pierces the working thread each time.

Starting left, a loop hangs between two higher points while the needle emerges at the centre below. Hold the loop flat with the thumb (left). A small stitch ties the loop and another stitch starts left (right). The tie can be any length and the entire stitch combines readily to form borders and all-over patterns.

Feather stitch   ## Double feather stitch

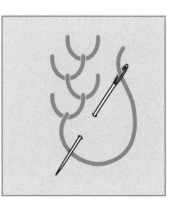

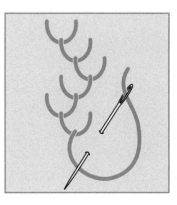

Stitch alternately to left and right. Always slant the needle in towards the centre while holding the thread down with the thumb.

Similar to Single feather stitch, with two additional stitches worked either side of the stitch line.

CHAIN STITCHES

Chain stitch

A looped stitch that works both as outline and filling. Constructs well with three or more strands of embroidery cotton [floss].

Bring needle through and insert again beside exit hole, leaving a loop on top. Bring needle up again through the loop, below the starting point. Pull gently until loop forms a rounded link. Repeat.

Detached chain (daisy) stitch

A quick stitch for depicting flowers and leaves, this variation on the chain loop can be made to form a circle of as many petals as you wish.

1 Begin as for chain stitch but work only one loop.

2 Make a small tying stitch to hold loop at its widest point. Needle through again at start of next petal.

A delicate Edwardian design for embroidery with daisy stitch and stem or split stitch. Ideal for use on a table or bed linen project, either as a single-unit corner-piece or linked in a ring.

Chequered chain

Thread needle with two colours and work alternate chain stitches with them. Take care to keep the unused thread above the needle point.

Tête de boeuf

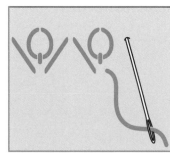

A detached chain stitch is set between two small straight stitches made in a V shape.

Broad chain

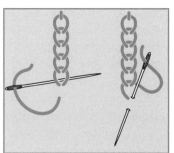

Reversed chain stitch, best worked fairly small. Start with a vertical running stitch. Pass needle back through it without piercing the fabric (left). Form chain link by taking stitch in fabric (right) and repeat.

Open chain

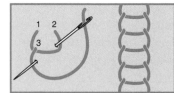

Keep needle slanted (left). The more horizontal it is, the wider and shallower the chain link (right). Stitch benefits from added ornamentation.

Back-stitched chain

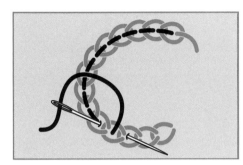

Make a foundation chain. Using a different-coloured thread if desired, needle up at centre of second chain stitch and back down into the first, coming up again through the third.

Whipped chain

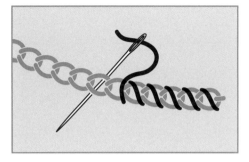

When the second thread is whipped over the total width and pulled tightly, the chain resembles a cord.

Raised band chain stitch

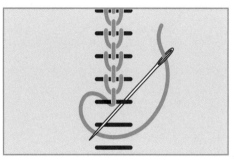

Worked over a foundation of closely spaced straight stitches, the chain stitch completes the band without piercing the fabric.

Coral zigzag stitch

Working from left to right between two parallel lines (drawn or tacked [basted]), make the first loop left like a chain stitch with crossed arms. Bring needle out through the loop, pull to form a knot and repeat to the right. These stitches should be worked close together.

Slipped chain stitch

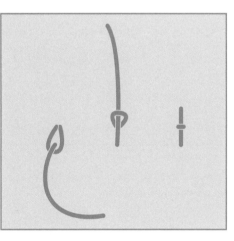

Make a single chain (left) but instead of a tying stitch, pull the thread in the opposite direction (centre), simultaneously tightening the loop to a small flat tie. Needle in to complete (right). Often used to highlight an outline.

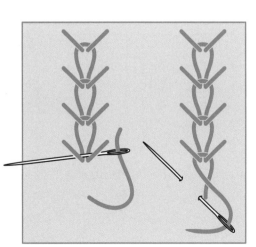

Wheatear stitch

Draw or tack [baste] a vertical line for guidance and make two straight stitches inwards, forming a right-angled V. Needle out again on the line, about 6 mm [¼ in] below. Slide needle through V without piercing the fabric (left). Needle in again to make a loop and out again ready to repeat (right).

BUTTONHOLE STITCHES AND SCROLL STITCH

Blanket stitch

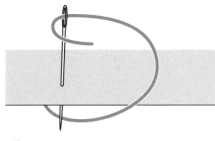

1 Secure thread on WS and bring through at fabric edge. Needle in at desired stitch height and width to the right. Needle out again directly below.

2 Pass the needle forwards through the loop, forming a half-hitch, and tighten the thread against the fabric edge. Repeat to form a row.

Coral stitch

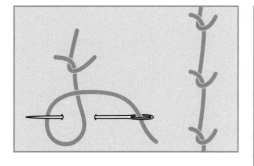

Hold thread taut and push needle in and out of the fabric either side of the thread (left). Pull through the resulting loop until a knot is formed. Repeat at regular intervals (right), either in straight lines or curved.

Wheel buttonhole (ring)

Work buttonhole stitch in a circle on a firmly woven fabric.

Buttonhole stitch

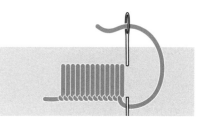

With the same basic construction as blanket stitch, this stitch evolved to seal the raw edges of a buttonhole. Stitched closely like satin stitch (p. 32), it can be used to neaten both straight and curved edges and features in cutwork embroidery like broderie anglaise (p. 48).

Scroll

Make a loop to the right and take a tiny vertical stitch within it. Pull thread through to complete the scroll. Make another loop to the right and repeat in a straight line. Looks better in twisted rather than stranded thread.

Double buttonholed bar

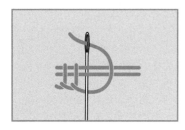

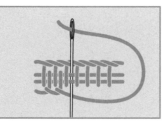

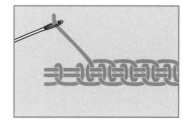

1 Lay two or three long stitches, using a tapestry needle and firm twist thread. Work one pass of well-spaced buttonhole stitch.

2 Turn and work a second row, dovetailing the verticals.

3 A variation made by looping across two verticals.

CRETAN STITCHES

Cretan stitch

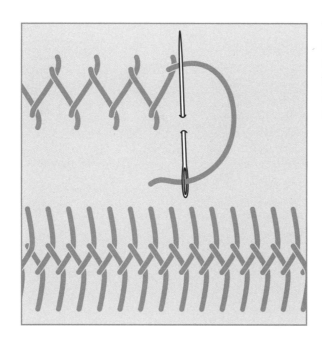

The stitches may be worked wide-spaced (top) or close together (bottom). They make good border stitches as well as fillings. The crossing effect is achieved by keeping the thread on the outside of the needle at every stitch.

Cretan open filling

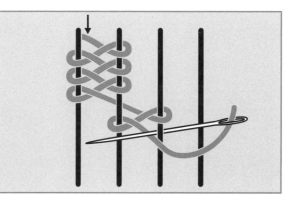

1 Lay a foundation of strong threads. The Cretan stitch is worked without piercing the fabric, except for starting and finishing points.

2 The stitch is worked diagonally in groups of four.

INSERTION STITCH

Faggoting (twisted insertion)

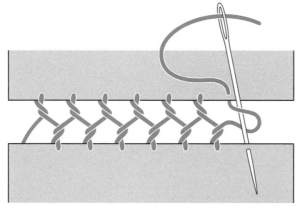

Take the two edges to be joined and lay them parallel to each other before tacking [basting] both onto strong backing paper. Work from left to right. Bring needle through lower edge and insert into top edge from back to front, a little to the right. Twist needle under and over thread across the gap, then insert into lower edge from back to front, again to the right. Repeat to the end, remove paper.

FILLING STITCHES

Satin (damask) stitch

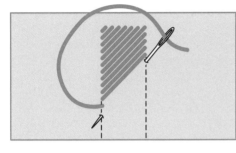

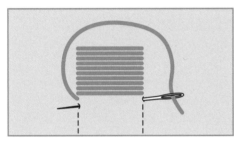

Satin stitch probably originated in China, to complement their beautiful silk threads. Work stitches very closely together to cover fabric completely. Needle in and out at the same angle within a defined outline.

This Chinese swallow design can be worked in sections of satin stitch. For a subtle sheen, try using twisted silk embroidery thread rather than six-stranded cotton [floss]. Arrange the birds in mirrored pairs, or six or seven in a circle.

Long and short satin stitch

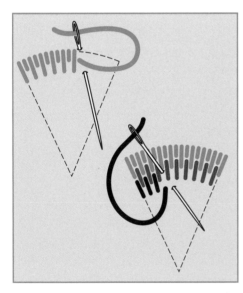

Using a frame, work the first row in alternate, distinctly long and short satin stitches, following your outlined shape (left). Dovetail subsequent rows in equal length stitches (right), using different colours for a shaded effect.

Brick filling

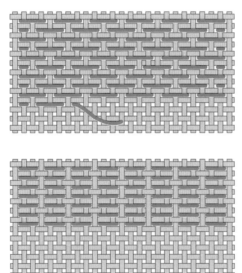

Work to and fro either vertically or horizontally on evenly woven fabric. Edges consist of long and short running stitches (top). Subsequent stitches are of equal length and parallel. Otherwise, arrange running stitch in columns (bottom). Both versions require even tension.

Brick and cross filling

1 Work groups of four satin stitches either vertically or horizontally, allowing equal spaces for the cross stitch.

2 Make sure that all the top stitches of the crosses go in one direction.

Surface darning

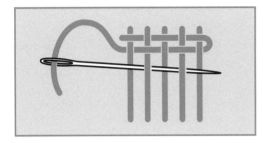

Lay a foundation of vertical threads and, without piercing the fabric except at starting and finishing points, weave top thread to and fro horizontally. If desired, use different colours to create woven patterns.

Trellis couched filling

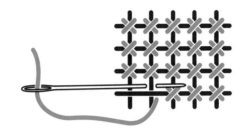

Work a grid of long, evenly spaced straight stitches. In a second colour, if desired, bring needle through at each intersection and work a cross stitch. A good filler for blackwork.

Roumanian stitch

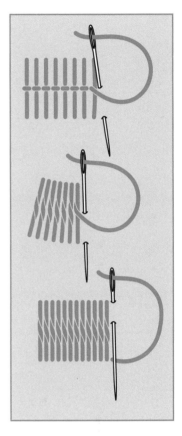

A good substitute for satin stitch, and very versatile in terms of spacing and arrangement in blocks, fans and so on. Long vertical stitches are tied down by the next stitch worked across, either horizontal (top) or diagonal.

Cloud filling

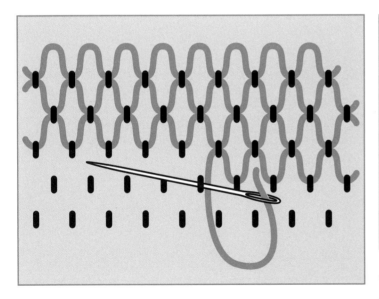

This stitch is best done with twist or pearl thread. Work regular rows of small vertical stitches, alternately spaced. Lace a second colour through foundation stitches, without piercing the fabric. Two loops meet under each vertical stitch. Alternatively, lace with narrow ribbon.

Ermine stitch

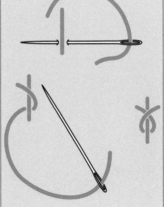

Work long, straight stitch (top) and tie with a cross. Space stitches evenly, with crosses wider at the top than at base.

COUCHING STITCHES

Couching is a technique in which one (heavier) thread is laid on the surface of the fabric and sewn into position by a different (finer) one. It is an economical method that helps rare or costly threads go further since they stay on the surface and are not 'wasted' on the wrong side; and if the ground fabric is delicate and the couched threads are heavy, neither is damaged in the process.

Couching stitches

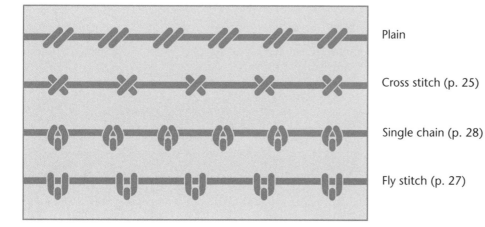

Plain

Cross stitch (p. 25)

Single chain (p. 28)

Fly stitch (p. 27)

Tied cross stitch

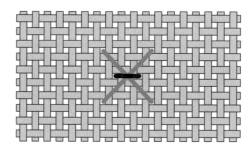

On an evenly woven fabric, work a cross stitch and bring needle through, level with centre. Make one straight stitch across centre. If desired, do a foundation row of cross stitch, then stitch central ties with a row of running stitch in a second colour.

Bokhara

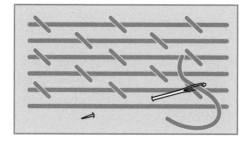

The couched thread should be laid down fairly slack and held by small, evenly spaced stitches, which are pulled tightly over the foundation thread. This is also a simple, rapid way of producing a solid filling, in which case the couching is worked in slanting lines with tying stitches alternately spaced, row by row.

SMOCKING STITCHES

Smocking is a traditional form of hand embroidery, worked over small folds of evenly gathered pre-shrunk fabric (allow three to four times the final width). When the gathering threads are removed the result is quite stretchy, making it ideal for use on children's clothes. For inclusion in soft furnishings, panels of smocked silk, linen or velvet look luxurious on cushion [pillow] covers.

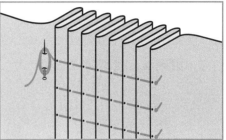

1 Unless you are smocking a gingham or stripe, where the pattern provides a guide, you will have to iron a transfer of smocking dots onto the wrong side of your fabric and with the grain. Stitch between the dots as shown, using contrasting thread that will be easy to remove.

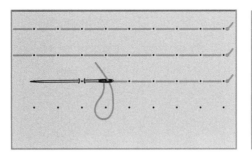

2 Pull up the gathering threads, not too tightly. Tie in pairs or wrap around pins, keeping fabric to the desired width. Make sure gathers are even. Embroider across the fronts of the folds. Use stranded embroidery cotton [floss] but work with only three strands at a time in an embroidery needle (p. 10).

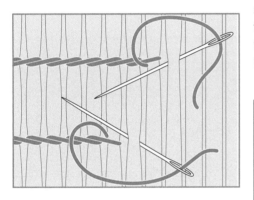

Stem stitch Because smocking is meant to be fairly elastic, try not to work too tightly. Make your first row in this simple stitch to test and establish your tension.

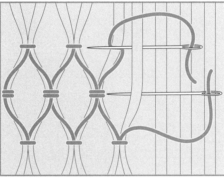

Surface honeycomb A stitch with plenty of stretch. Back stitch across two folds, needle out between them, drop 6 mm [¼ in] and enter next right-hand fold from right to left, back stitch again. Repeat sequence, going up and down alternately. Invert lower line to form honeycomb pattern. Always check thread is correctly above or below needle.

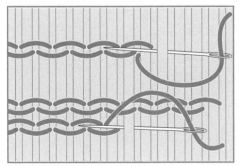

Cable stitch A firm stitch. Needle out through first fold left, thread below needle and stitch over second fold, bringing needle out between first and second. Work with thread above and below needle alternately. Double cable stitch is two rows of cable worked together so they reflect each other.

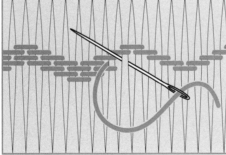

Double closed wave A firm stitch. While making one set of steps upwards, slant the needle up slightly and keep thread below it. On the downward steps, slant the needle down and keep thread above it. A second or third row is made to fit into the zigzags, either close together, as shown, or spaced.

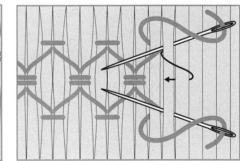

Diamond stitch A large, stretchy stitch that encloses two folds. Needle out on second line, up to first. Back stitch over first fold and then the second with thread above needle. Needle down to second line. Back stitch third fold, then the fourth with thread below. Needle up to fifth fold and repeat. Start second stage on the third line, to complete the shape.

A BACK STITCH ALPHABET

A sampler-style alphabet with matching numerals, designed to be executed in back stitch using just two or three strands of embroidery cotton [floss].

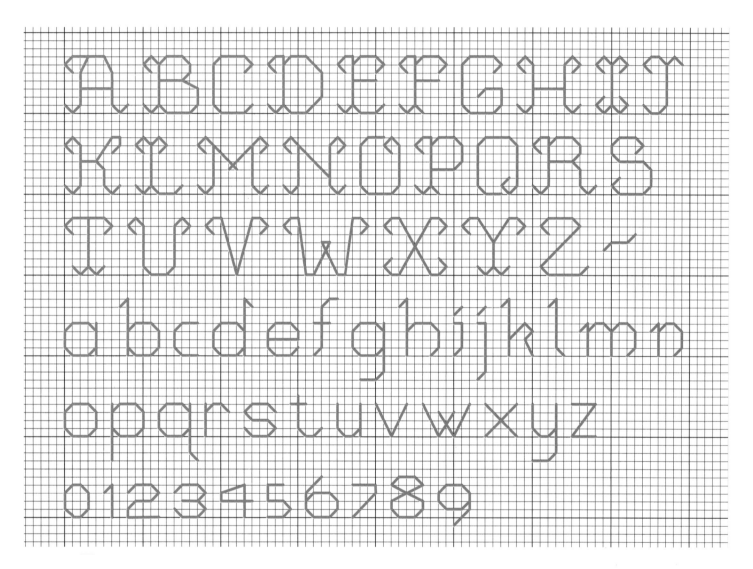

This alphabet is not only for samplers, it is also suitable for lettering embroidered greetings cards or for signing and dating your own projects. Use it as a guide for other stitches when working monograms onto pockets, covered buttons or handkerchiefs, and to personalize gift items such as bookmarks, key fobs, wallets and phone cases.

MAKE AND EMBROIDER A SOFT TOY ELEPHANT

Decorate this toy elephant with your own embroidery designs and transform her into one of the stars of the Elephant Festival.

If you intend to embroider the head gusset it should be done before cutting the shape from the contrast fabric (indicated by a coloured dot on the pattern piece). Use an embroidery hoop if you wish.

The saddle cloth – or jhool – is a separate piece of material, measuring 23 x 9.5 cm [9 x 3¾ in], it can be any fabric you choose, so long as it is suitable for stitching, and can be secured to the elephant's back when finished. You could make it into a type of sampler using your favourite stitches (see p. 138 for border patterns). Or with such a festive subject , you could take your inspiration from Indian embroidery itself, perhaps attempting some shisha work (p. 52).

Add decorative silky cord, fringing and tassels as final touches.

Although the basic elephant pattern makes up into a safe toy, and embroidery alone would provide no risk, the addition of beads, sequins, cord, tassels or anything that may become detached from the toy would make it unsuitable for young children.

Tassels

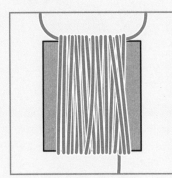

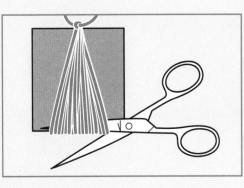

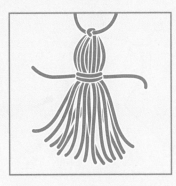

1 Wrap the thread around the card. Thread one strand, 30 cm [12 in] long, under the top loops.

2 Tie this strand tightly at the top; the ends can be knotted or twisted later, or threaded up for sewing. Cut all the tassel loops free at the lower edge.

3 Take another length of thread and wind firmly round the loose strands to form the tassel head. Finish with a secure knot. Thread the ends into a needle and work neatly into the centre of the tassel before trimming level.

TOY ELEPHANT [continued]

HEIGHT: 18 cm [7 in] **LENGTH:** 25.5 cm [10 in]   **LEVEL: ADVANCED**

Note: Because of the complex seaming required and the fact that the elephant needs very firm filling, you are advised to use a sewing machine throughout.

YOU WILL NEED

Main body fabric 65 x 40 cm
[25½ x 16 in] – close-woven is best

Contrast fabric 65 x 25 cm
[25½ x 10 in] for gussets and ear lining – close-woven is best

60 cm [24 in] black embroidery thread for tail

Two small black buttons for eyes

Filling

Cut out all the pattern pieces. There is a 5 mm [³⁄₁₆ in] seam allowance.

1 In the contrast fabric, sew half the body gusset to the inner front and rear leg sections, from B to A and from C to D.

2 Repeat with the other half of the body gusset.

3 Pin and tack [baste] the two body gusset assemblies right sides (RS) together, then stitch from E to G. Clip the curve.

4 Take two ear pieces, one of each fabric, and place RS together. Tack [baste] and sew around the curve from K to L, leaving the straight side open for turning.

5 Repeat for the second ear. Clip the curves and turn both ears RS out.

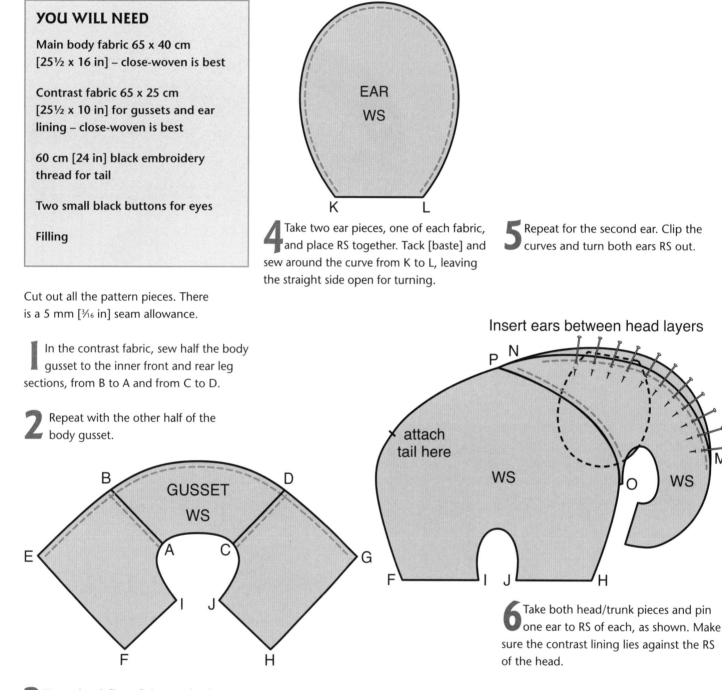

6 Take both head/trunk pieces and pin one ear to RS of each, as shown. Make sure the contrast lining lies against the RS of the head.

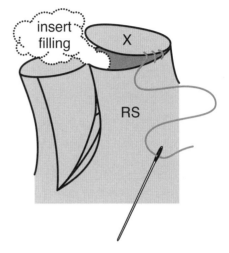

7 Pin the head gusset to the top curve of one side of the head from N to M, including the ear.

8 Repeat, joining the other head/trunk section to the other side of the head gusset.

9 Tack [baste] and then stitch the head to the main body on both sides, from points O to P.

10 Tack [baste] and sew each side of the head gusset from M to N.

11 RS together, sew the body gusset to the body side round the arch from I to J. Clip the curve.

12 Repeat, joining the other body side to the opposite side of the gusset.

13 Sew down all four legs from points E to F and G to H.

14 Cut three 20 cm [8 in] strands of embroidery thread for the tail. Tie a knot in one end and plait as far as you wish before tying off with a knot and leaving a tassel end.

15 Insert the tail centrally on the back seam, as indicated, with only the base knot sticking out. The rest of the tail should be on the inside for now.

16 Tack [baste] and sew the two body sides together down the spine from P to E. Remove all tacking [basting].

17 Sew the soles of three of the feet into the leg holes, RS facing inwards, matching points H and J, and F and I. With one sole only (see X), sew half the pad to the leg and leave a gap for turning and filling.

18 Turn the whole elephant RS out through the foot hole.

19 Fill firmly, starting with the elephant's trunk. Use a stuffing stick to reach the tip of the trunk and fill it up solidly into the head gusset. The feet and legs should be tightly stuffed too, to avoid sagging where they join the body.

20 Oversew neatly to close the gap in the fourth foot.

21 Attach small black buttons for the eyes.

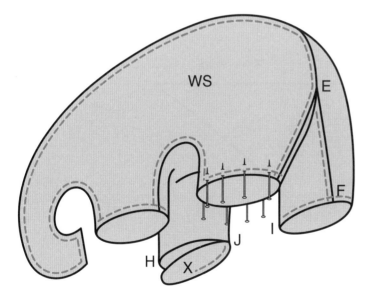

ELEPHANT

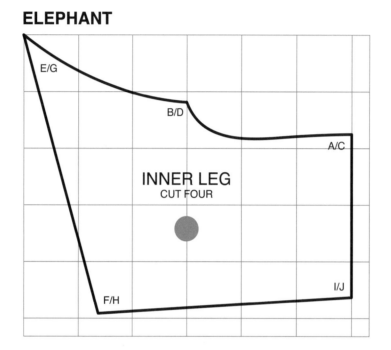

INNER LEG
CUT FOUR

E/G

B/D

A/C

F/H

I/J

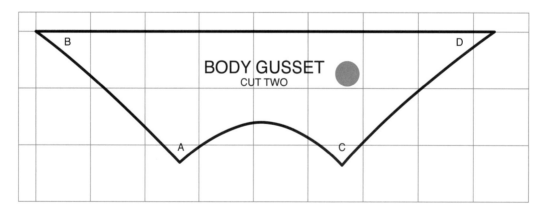

BODY GUSSET
CUT TWO

B

A

C

D

ELEPHANT

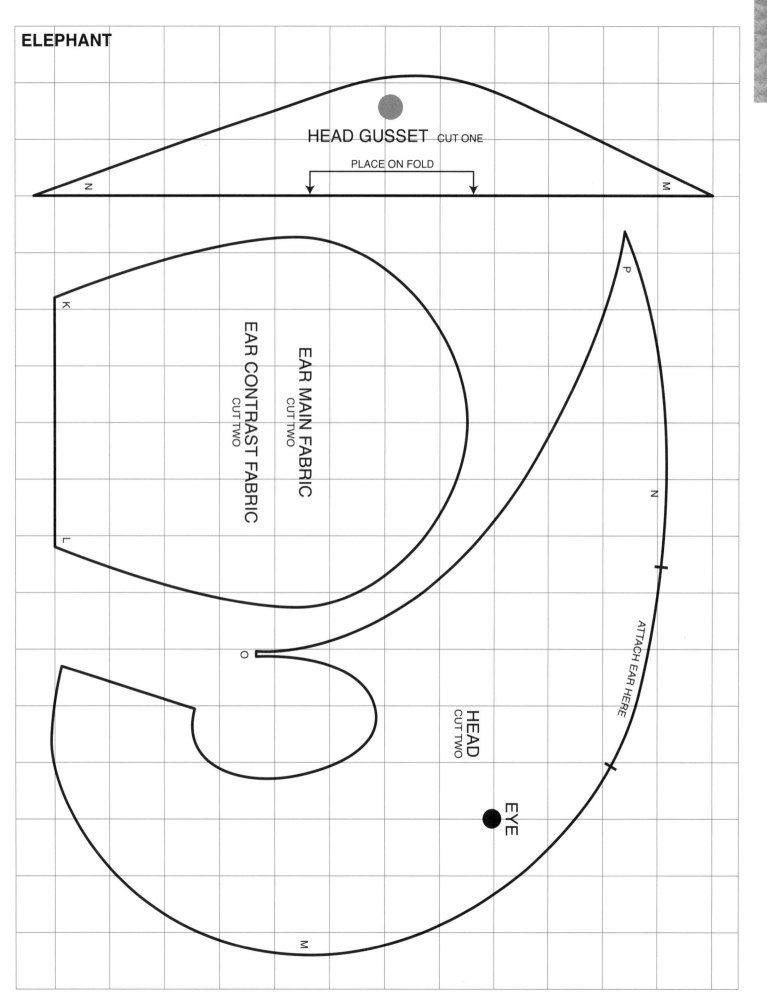

HEAD GUSSET CUT ONE

PLACE ON FOLD

N

M

K

EAR CONTRAST FABRIC
CUT TWO

EAR MAIN FABRIC
CUT TWO

L

P

N

ATTACH EAR HERE

O

HEAD
CUT TWO

EYE

M

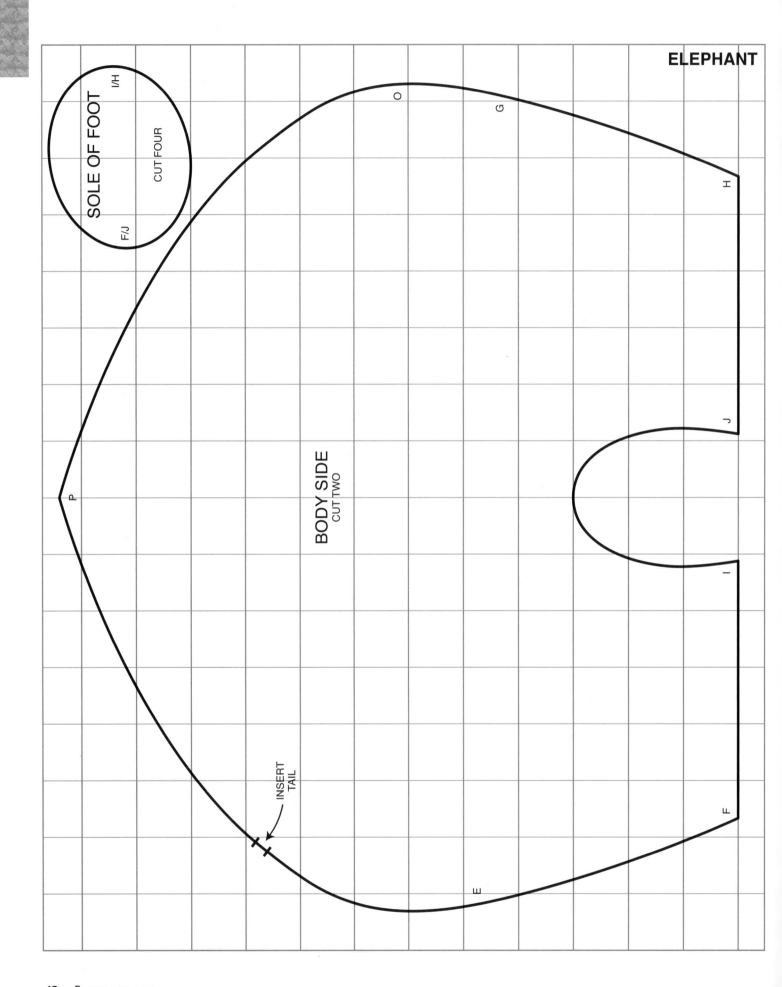

SOLE OF FOOT

I/H

CUT FOUR

F/J

O

G

H

J

P

BODY SIDE
CUT TWO

I

INSERT
TAIL

F

E

PART THREE

MACHINE EMBROIDERY METHODS AND TECHNIQUES

THE SEWING MACHINE

A well-built sewing machine will give years of service so long as it is properly used and maintained.

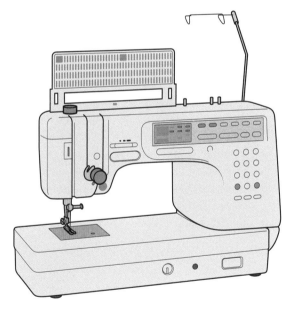

Threading the machine

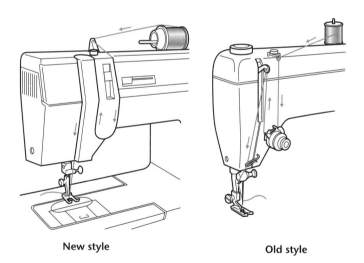

New style

Old style

As a beginner or occasional sewer, look no further than a basic electric model that sews different sizes of straight, hem, stretch and zigzag stitches at the twist of a dial, and a good range of decorative stitches too.

Computerized sewing machines (shown above) are controlled by microchips and several internal motors, making them extremely versatile as well as more expensive. Operated via a touch screen and LCD display, they can memorize and reproduce past tasks and offer hundreds of different stitches, fonts and designs via downloads from a PC.

Newer-style machines incorporate tension discs, thread guides and a take-up lever inside the casing, which eliminates a number of steps involved in threading older models. Consult the manufacturer's manual. If you have no printed instructions, search for your make and model on the web, where a huge range of manuals is available. Be aware that some needles thread from front to back and some from left to right. Incorrect threading is probably responsible for more beginners' problems than anything else. Always raise the presser foot while threading the machine and lower it when putting it away.

Needle, presser foot, feed-dogs, needle plate

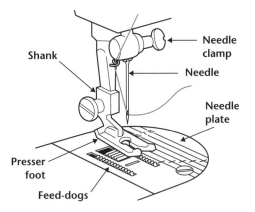

Shank · Needle clamp · Needle · Needle plate · Presser foot · Feed-dogs

Ordinary machine needles are available in sizes 60-130 [8-19]; keep spare sets and change frequently. Avoid bending or breaking them by raising the needle clear before removing work and don't drag while stitching. The finest needle will stitch delicates and the thickest is for tough fabrics like twill. Fit a ballpoint needle for knits or stretch fabrics; use a large-eyed, sharp topstitch needle to take thicker thread and pierce multiple layers.

The presser foot holds the fabric flat against the feed-dogs while the needle makes the stitch. Feed-dogs have tiny metal teeth that move the fabric from front to back as stitching proceeds. The needle plate fits over the feed-dogs, covering the bobbin, with a hole for the tip of the needle to pass through. In free-motion stitching (with or without a presser foot) the feed-dogs are lowered or covered, allowing the fabric to be moved about manually, often while held taut in a hoop.

Five useful machine feet for embroiderers

  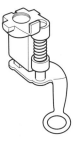  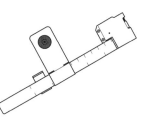

1 Straight-stitch The general purpose presser foot that comes ready to use on most sewing machines.

2 Zigzag Has a horizontal slot for the 'swing' of the needle as it forms a zigzag with the thread. Use this foot with multiple needles but do not attempt zigzag stitch with them.

3 Embroidery/ darning Use in free-motion embroidery together with lowered feed-dogs and hooped fabric. Allows manoeuvrability of fabric and close control of stitching while protecting the fingers.

4 Walking/quilting Uses teeth to feed upper and lower layers of fabric together evenly and avoid bunching. Also ideal for vinyl, velvets and fabrics that tend to slip or stretch.

5 Circular sewing attachment A sliding attachment fixes the radius with a slotted pin to hold the centre of the fabric while a perfect circle is worked in the chosen stitch.

Speciality needles

1 Twin needle Requires two spools of top thread but interlocks with a single bobbin. The effect is two equidistant stitch lines on top and a zigzag beneath. Can be used only where the top threading system is from front to back and the needle plate has a hole wide enough. Triple needles are also available.

2 Wing needle The blade on each side of the needle pushes open the weave of the fabric where the needle penetrates. Creates decorative effects resembling drawn thread work.

Bobbin

The bobbin holds the lower thread. It lies next to the needle plate, in a compartment with a sliding lid. Fluff [lint] collects here and should be brushed out often. Lower thread tension is controlled by a small screw that regulates the spring on the bobbin case. Certain techniques and types of thread require altered tension. If you use them regularly, keep two or three cases adjusted to different tensions, rather than constantly tightening and loosening the same one.

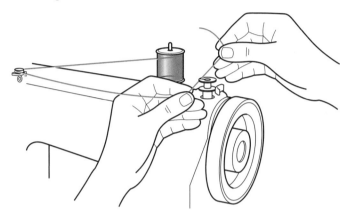

The bobbin is filled automatically from the winder on the machine, which ensures it is evenly wound under tension. Some bobbins can be filled in situ under the plate.

This type sits vertically in the bobbin race and is released by a latch on the case. When replaced, the thread should slot under the spring with a tail of 10 cm [4 in].

The 'drop-in' type sits horizontally beneath the plate. There is usually an angled slot to pull the bobbin thread through.

Thread tension

Regular machine stitching is formed by the top and lower threads interlocking in the fabric. Creative machine embroiderers manipulate thread tension for deliberate effects.

1 Top thread tension is governed by the tension dial, numbered 0–9. Behind it, the thread runs between two or three discs that are adjusted according to the dial.

2 Between 4 and 5 on the dial is considered 'normal' tension. The threads meet in the centre of the fabric and the stitching appears the same on each side.

3 Below 4, the tension discs loosen and the top thread runs more freely. The thread can then pass through both layers of fabric. You can create gathers on a long stitch setting by pulling up the bottom thread.

4 Above 5, the discs are screwed together more tightly and the reverse happens.

Stitch length and width

Stitch length is measured in millimetres from 1 to 6 and controlled by a dial or lever on the front of the machine. This activates the feed-dogs. Use the longest stitches (4-6 mm [⅛-¼ in]) for heavyweight fabrics, topstitching, gathering and tacking [basting]. Medium length stitches (2.5-4 mm [³⁄₃₂-⅛ in]) are suitable for mid-weight fabrics. Fine fabrics use a 2 mm [1⁄16 in] stitch. A row of 1 mm [1⁄32 in] stitches is difficult to unpick so try to be sure of what you are doing when using the smallest.

Stitch width does not apply to straight stitching. The width control – also found on the front of the machine – sets the 'swing' of the needle when working zigzag or other decorative stitches. The measurement is in millimetres and usually goes up to 6 mm [¼ in]. For free-motion embroidery, try setting the machine for a wide zigzag and stitch fast to produce a satin effect.

USING HOOPS AND STABILIZERS

The manufacturers of computerized machines supply hoops and frames that move automatically to produce pre-programmed patterns. However it is possible to achieve impressive results using only a basic machine and the sprung version of a hand embroidery hoop.

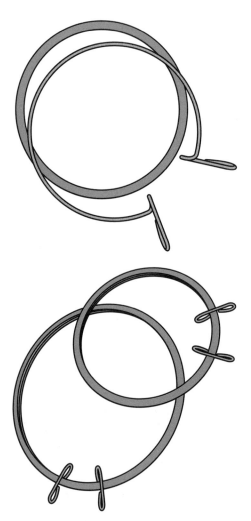

Sprung hoops

This slim hoop slides under the machine foot and handles well during free-motion stitching. The sprung clip fits on the inside of the hoop and holds the fabric really taut. It is quick and easy to change projects or to move the hoop around a large fabric area.

It is worth pointing out that the traditional wooden hoop also works with machine embroidery, the only difference being that the rim is turned uppermost so that the wrong side of the fabric rests flat against the base plate.

You can avoid hoop marks on your fabric by fixing a sheet of one-sided adhesive stabilizer tightly into the hoop itself. Peel off the backing within the hoop and stick the fabric flat to the stabilizer. Densely stitched designs will require a heavy support to ensure the work doesn't pucker, while lighter pieces should not be made too stiff.

Stabilizers

Stabilizers are used above or below the fabric – with or without a hoop – to prevent it shifting or stretching while machining. There are various kinds, from paper, cotton and open mesh to nylon and polyvinyl alcohol. The 'tear away' or 'cut away' sort is removed once the stitching is complete, retained only on the back of the stitched area itself. This type is frequently used for T-shirts, knits and synthetic fabrics. Another type is a smooth non-woven cotton stabilizer, available plain or as an 'iron-on' for stretch fabrics.

There is an easy-tear, cold-water soluble stabilizer designed for fleeces and lightweight delicates. There is also a heavyweight version, ideal for complex free-motion embroidery and – when used without any base fabric at all – it offers embroiderers the exciting chance to produce pure lace or filigree work.

For any project that cannot be wetted or is too delicate to withstand tearing, choose the heat-sensitive vanishing muslin that obligingly disintegrates under a dry iron or in a moderate oven and can be brushed away. Finally, there is a hot-water soluble fabric that can be three-dimensionally moulded if sufficient residue is allowed to remain after boiling.

TECHNIQUES TO TRY

Practising a technique or element of design encourages you to develop your ideas instead of rigidly following a pattern. Experiment with the threads and fabric you want to use – glossy, matt or metallic – as your choice can alter the whole look and purpose of a piece.

Regular pattern

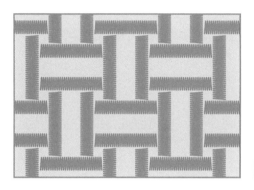

Work wide zigzag stitch in short parallel lines vertically and horizontally. Try this on coarse canvas and then velvet – the results will be very different.

Uneven tension

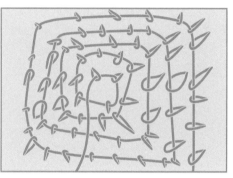

Work a straight-stitched spiral with the top thread tension too tight and the bottom too loose. Try different colours for the top thread and bobbin.

Textures

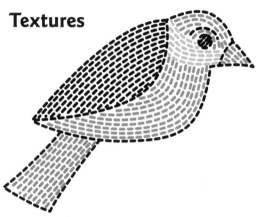

Fill areas with regular rows of straight stitch in different threads and colours. Needle down at the end of a row, raise the foot and turn the fabric through 180 degrees before lowering the foot again.

Filling patterns

Sashiko A filling pattern carried out in long, straight stitch. Use a white twist thread on a dark fabric to echo Japanese Sashiko style.

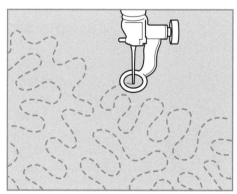

Free motion machining in straight stitch with an embroidery/darning foot and the feed-dogs lowered. Stitch fast but move the hoop slowly and smoothly with both hands. Jerky movements make uneven stitches.

Decorated initials

A formal satin-stitched initial superimposed with freestyle decoration. Create twigs from cord made by zigzagging over a core of string or yarn, pulled steadily through the machine.

TWO SPECIAL EFFECTS

Cutwork and appliqué are two stitching techniques that can be done by either hand or machine. The latter can save time on a large project.

CUTWORK

Machine eyelet border

Eyelet, whitework and broderie anglaise are all variations of cutwork and look best stitched in glossy thread on a matt cotton base. A pattern is marked out on the fabric and defined with two lines of straight stitch plus one more line run between them for 'padding' before embroidery begins.

Eyelet embroidery foot

The embroidery is worked around a punched hole in a close zigzag or Satin stitch. Vertical spring action of the foot stops the fabric lifting with the needle and gives consistent stitching, even at speed.

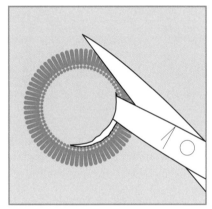

Turn to WS and cut the fabric off as close as possible to the base of the buttonhole stitch.

The smallest eyelets are made with scissor points. One round of stay stitch is followed by buttonhole pulled firmly away from the centre, or simply oversewing to neaten the edge.

APPLIQUÉ

Appliqué foot

The toes on this foot are shorter than the usual zigzag foot, for smoother stitching and greater manoeuvrability. It is particularly suited for satin stitching, appliqué and couching.

Machine stitched appliqué

It is hard to sew appliqué down flat without a margin. Draw the final outline on the chosen fabric, cut it out with a normal seam allowance and tack [baste] to the background. Machine along the drawn line with a straight stitch and cut off excess fabric as close as possible to the stitched line. With even tension top and bottom, set to zigzag around the shape. Stitch fast to produce a satin stitch but move the fabric slowly so the stitching is controlled and covers the raw edges.

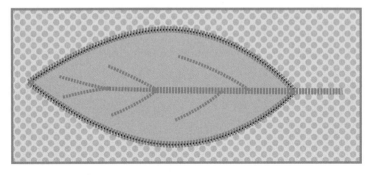

MOTIFS

Here are a few motifs suitable for adaptation to machine embroidery. Try stitching the spirals free-motion in a hoop and see how you can expand them into intricate filling patterns. The solid shapes can also be scaled up for appliqué work.

PROJECT: BAG KEEPER

Keep plastic carriers tidy and ready to re-use in this neat bag keeper.

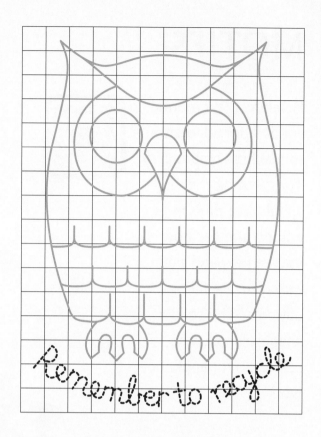

Materials

- Fabric for the embroidered label, cut to any size or shape you wish. With thick felt you probably won't need backing, otherwise, cut iron-on Vilene or stabilizer to fit
- Cotton fabric for the bag itself, 51 x 63.5 cm [20 x 25 in]
- Elastic 7 mm [¼ in] wide, cut into two lengths, 30 cm [12 in] and 15 cm [6 in]
- Ribbon or tape for the handle, 37.5 cm [15 in] long, 20 mm [¾ in] wide
- You will also need a sewing machine, needles, threads, bodkin, scissors and an iron

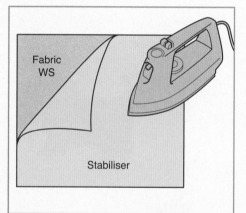

Fabric WS

Stabiliser

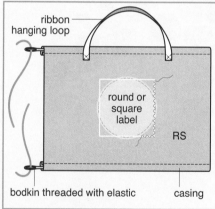

ribbon hanging loop

round or square label

RS

bodkin threaded with elastic

casing

1 Attach the Vilene or stabilizer to the label fabric. The elephant image can be squared up for either embroidery or appliqué. You might like to trace your own handwriting on embroiderer's carbon paper, or copy the alphabet (p. 36). If you prefer hand embroidery, you could make the elephant into a sampler of your favourite stitches or stitch it in a regional style. In that case, hoop the fabric for embroidering and interface with Vilene only when finished.

2 Take the bag fabric and make a 13 mm [½ in] casing on both long sides by first folding over 20 mm [¾ in] and then turning the raw edge under again by 7 mm [¼ in]. Tack (baste) the turning and machine stitch the casings, close to the fold.

3 Measure and pin your label to the centre. Attach it with a decorative machine stitch or plain topstitch. Fold in the raw ends of the ribbon and sew the handle firmly near the top edge, about 17.5 cm [7 in] from either end and below the casing.

4 With the bodkin, run the 30 cm [12 in] elastic through the top casing, gathering fabric as you go. Sew down the ends close to each edge. Repeat with the bottom casing, using the 15 cm [6 in] elastic. The opening at the bottom is narrower than the top.

WS

5 Fold the bag in half lengthways, wrong side out. With a 13 mm [½ in] seam allowance, machine the side seam from top to bottom, ensuring that the ends of the elastic are firmly included. Press the seam smooth if necessary.

6 Turn the bag right side out and hang up ready for use.

PART FOUR:
REGIONAL EMBROIDERY

THE INDIAN TRADITION

From a prime position on land and maritime trade routes between China and Europe, India has gathered a rich tradition of embroidery, especially in the north-west border region of Gujarat.

Printing blocks

The carrier of many Indian patterns and motifs is the simple hand-carved wooden printing block. More precise geometric patterns are printed from metal strips, hammered edge-on into the face of the wood. Both kinds are stamped onto the base fabric as a stitching guide.

Aari work

Chain stitch is worked in frames large and small (fabric tightly stretched and right side up) using either a needle or a small hooked awl called an aari, similar to the western tambour hook. With the thread held beneath the fabric, the hook is inserted downwards (a) and the thread caught, the hook turned and drawn upwards in a loop. With the hook above the fabric (b) and light tension on the lower thread, it is turned and inserted again at a short distance and another loop is drawn up through the centre of the previous one. With each action of the aari, the embroiderer twists it vertically through 180 degrees to hold the thread. Cotton, silk and wool are all used in aari work (see rear cover for an antique silk example from Gujarat, c. 1760).

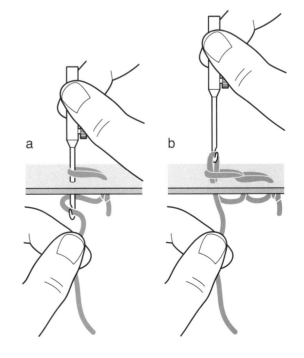

Shisha mirror work

Small, round, factory-made mirrors are the most commonly used; large sequins are an unbreakable alternative. Attach with a choice of stitches: buttonhole (p. 30), herringbone (p. 26), twisted chain (right) or Cretan (p. 31) or for a more elaborate effect, a combination of several. Slipped chain (p. 29) is frequently used last as a radiating outline.

Anchor the mirror to the fabric with two horizontal and two vertical stitches (a) and (b). Pass the needle under the first intersection, cross over and make a stitch from right to left (c). With even tension as you go, continue anti-clockwise until the frame is complete (d). An alternative method is to wrap a small ring with coloured thread, place it over the mirror and slip stitch firmly into place.

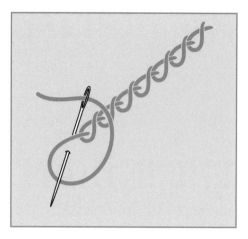

Twisted chain

A chain variation that gives a raised line and makes a useful addition to the texture of a Shisha surround.

Badla

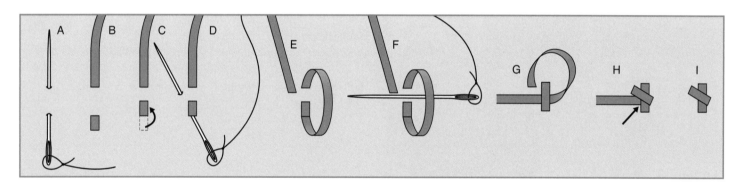

A metal embroidery technique that consists of producing tiny dots (fardi), and also very small eyelets and sequins that twinkle like stars on fine translucent materials such as voile, muslin and silk. The 'thread' is narrow strips of recycled metal approximately 2mm [¹⁄₁₆ in] wide and 30 cm [12 in] long.

Working in the hand, the special badla needle is threaded (A) and the metal pulled through the ground fabric until a short tail is left. This is bent over to secure it (B and C). The needle is inserted again (D) and pulled through to make a loop (E). It is then passed through the loop (F) and the metal strip forms a cross (G). The strip is pulled flush to the fabric and broken off (H). The fardi is complete (I). The Badla is finally burnished with a smooth stone.

Banjara

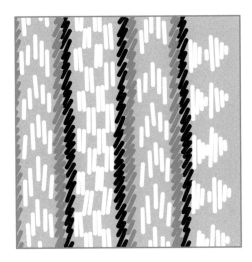

Banjara is the name given to the nomadic tribes of India. Their close-stitched, colourful, cotton-on-cotton embroidery is arranged in solid geometric patterns, making extensive use of straight and Florentine-style stitchwork.

Kantha

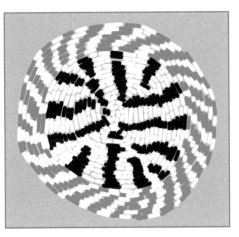

Kantha, meaning 'rags', is a style of cotton quilting from Bengal. Running stitch provides the basis combined with back, stem and split stitches, and pattern darning, to work a series of characteristic motifs.

Kutch cross stitch

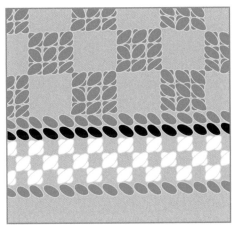

Minute cross stitch of such precision that it almost appears woven. This work is easier carried out by the counted thread method on an evenly woven fabric

Shadow work with closed herringbone

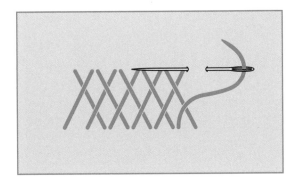

Shadow work is an element of the Indian whitework technique called Chikan. Worked on the wrong side of transparent fabrics such as voile and organza, the closed herringbone produces two lines of back stitch on the front.

Double back stitch (shadow work)

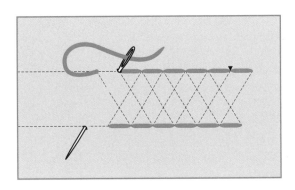

The back stitch on the right side of shadow work forms a continuous outline to the herringbone filling. The crosses show through the fabric, creating a distinct tonal variation.

PROJECT: PEACOCK CUSHION COVER

The cushion cover is assembled from recycled pieces of block-printed cotton and silk, appliquéd with an embroidered peacock motif. Printed fabrics always add character and speak of the time and part of the world they belong to, see a similar project shown on the rear cover.

Select fabrics of matching weight, choosing colours and prints that coordinate with one another. Iron well before cutting out each patch; include a 13mm [½ in] seam allowance.

Right sides facing, machine stitch the pieces together in blocks as shown below. Once finished, press seams on the wrong side.

Scale up (p. 11), draw and cut the peacock shape from a bright, contrasting fabric; keep a margin of 13mm [½ in].

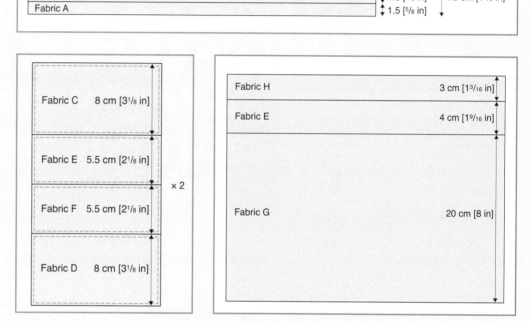

Fabric A	↕ 1.5 [⅝ in]
Fabric B x 2	↕ 1.5 [⅝ in]
Fabric A	↕ 1.5 [⅝ in]

4.5 cm [1⅞ in]

Fabric C   8 cm [3⅛ in]

Fabric E   5.5 cm [2⅛ in]

Fabric F   5.5 cm [2⅛ in]

Fabric D   8 cm [3⅛ in]

× 2

Fabric H   3 cm [1³/₁₆ in]

Fabric E   4 cm [1⁹/₁₆ in]

Fabric G   20 cm [8 in]

Attach the motif to the right side of the patchwork by hand with rows of running stitch in brightly coloured embroidery threads. Finally, outline with chain stitch.

Trim off the extra fabric close to the chain stitch. Draw on the tail feathers with a soluble marker. Fill them in using herringbone stitch in various colours and outline again with a contrasting chain stitch.

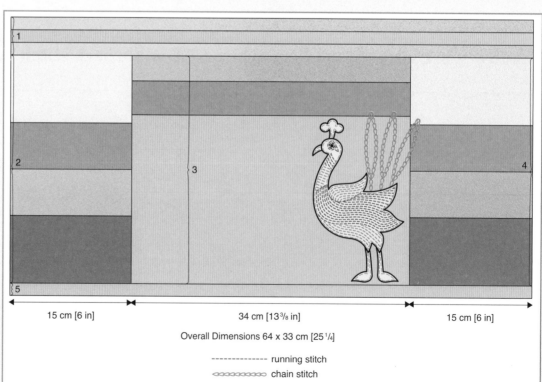

15 cm [6 in]   34 cm [13⅜ in]   15 cm [6 in]

Overall Dimensions 64 x 33 cm [25¼]

----------- running stitch

⊂⊃⊂⊃⊂⊃⊂⊃ chain stitch

THE PERUVIAN PARACAS

Some amazing 2000-year-old textiles came to light in the 1920s with the discovery of a vast necropolis on the Paracas peninsula. Each mummified body was ritually wrapped in layers of ornate embroideries.

Peruvian cat in stem stitch

The parading beasts, birds and strange flying figures (right and below) were meticulously worked in sections of close Stem stitch, covering the cotton base weave at different angles and lengths (see below right). The alpaca wool threads took the dyes well, so the array of purples, deep reds, pinks, yellows and greens remain vivid even now.

Flying figures

Monkey

Stem stitch formation

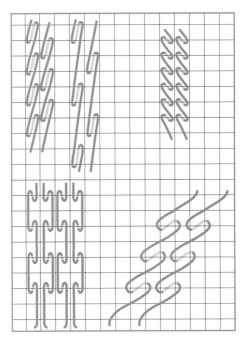

EUROPEAN FOLK EMBROIDERY

European embroidery has typically looked to linen and wool for everyday use, with most of the exquisite gold and silk examples reserved for the Church.

Russian cross stitch

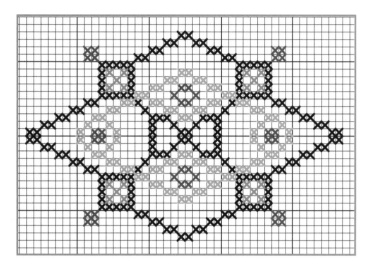

This four-colour motif was chosen to decorate a plain white glazed cotton apron. The grid pattern (above left) shows how the design is plotted for stitching over waste canvas. The canvas is tacked [basted] onto the cotton fabric and the cross stitch is worked through both layers simultaneously. When finished, the threads of the waste canvas are cut and withdrawn to leave the design intact on the plain ground (above right).

Hungarian 'written' embroidery

This is a much-enlarged section of a convoluted double chain-stitch pattern, worked in red twist on a white linen bag. The pattern is from Kalotaszeg in Transylvania, once part of Hungary. This traditional style is called 'written' embroidery, designed by the local Writing Woman, who memorizes hundreds of patterns and can draw them freehand, to order, on blank linen. Stylized floral motifs predominate and the stitch used is always one of the chain family, such as broad chain (p. 28), open chain (p. 28) or heavy chain (braid) stitch.

The bag itself is stitched together with blanket stitch in matching thread.

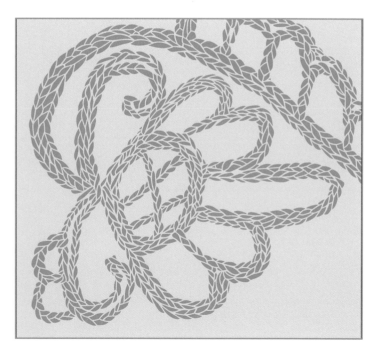

Apart from the nobility and town dwellers, for centuries most Europeans worked on the land. They also sewed their own clothes and household linen, which naturally led to decorating them too, usually with motifs and colours specific to their own communities. Existence was hard and nothing was allowed to go to waste. They would embroider only the parts of a garment that showed, like collars, sleeves and hems. Counted thread embroidery – chiefly cross stitch – is found everywhere from the 'dixos' (medallions) of the Greek islands to Scandinavia. Chain, stem, split and Cretan stitches gave embroiderers greater scope to create more flowing outlines and complex fillings.

Icelandic cross stitch

Crowned heart design.

Romanian chain and satin stitch

The sleeve motif from a folk costume.

Chinese satin stitch

Satin-weave fabric (p. 12) and satin stitch embroidery (p. 32) have long been used by the Chinese to show off the sheer beauty of their silk threads. The tomb of an aristocratic woman who died in 1243 CE yielded fabulous gold satin embroideries of flowering branches and perching birds. However, satin stitch had displaced chain stitch even earlier, in the Tang era (618–906 CE). And later, during the trading boom of the eighteenth and nineteenth centuries, most of the silk that China exported to the West was patterned with satin embroidery because such delicate designs were quicker and easier to produce by hand than via the complexities of loom weaving.

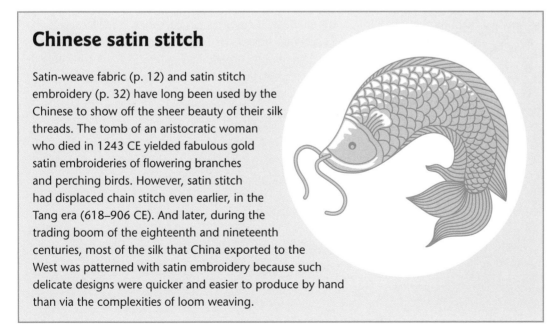

HARDANGER

During the seventeenth century, the Hardanger region of southern Norway adopted and gave its name to a much older kind of counted thread embroidery, also known as whitework, traditionally worked with threads matching a white or cream linen background.

Kloster blocks

Present-day Hardanger fabric takes the form of evenweave cotton, typically 22-count across both warp and weft (see also p. 127), which produces a square mesh with clear holes, making it easier to work than standard evenweaves. The embroidery thread generally used is perle (pearl), No 5 for blocks and a finer No 8 for fillings.

Because you can actually see through parts of Hardanger work, it seems complicated and difficult, and the fact that it involves cutting threads scares many stitchers. However, the secret is in learning to do the preparatory 5-stitch Kloster block well and to count correctly as you go.

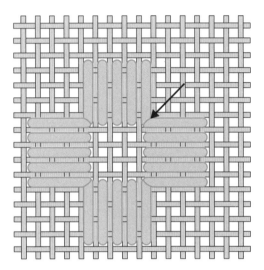

Hardanger

The chief rule is never to start cutting until the Kloster blocks are all done and you've checked that they match horizontally. A certain number of warp and weft threads are cut within the enclosed areas, then drawn out to leave a series of exposed threads and large holes.

Finally, various decorative stitches are worked over the remaining threads. Most characteristic of Hardanger are the woven and wrapped bars, the satin-stitched motifs, and the filling stitches that look like wheel and spider's webs.

The geometric shapes of traditional Hardanger can be built into wonderful patterns but there are also many opportunities for contemporary needleworkers to experiment with multi-coloured threads and modern settings.

WASHING AND MOUNTING

Washing embroidery

Most contemporary embroidery threads are colourfast, but if you have any doubts, press a damp cotton wool pad against the stitching (preferably on the wrong side). If it stains the cotton wool, the embroidery should be dry cleaned. Wash colourfast pieces in lukewarm water only with pure soap flakes. Squeeze gently and do not rub the stitching. Rinse in several changes of cool water before rolling the embroidery in a clean towel to remove excess water. Unwrap and gently pull the piece into shape. Dry away from direct heat or strong sunlight. If the piece has become distorted, 'block' it by stretching and pinning onto a soft board with long, rustproof pins around the edge. Leave until totally dry. Always iron face down on a padded surface, using a damp pressing cloth if necessary.

Mounting

Cut a mount from thin hardboard, mount board or foam board. Hardboard needs to be sawn but use a sharp craft knife for the others, together with a metal ruler and a cutting mat. Keep your fingers behind the cutting edge. To pad your work for display, cut the wadding [batting] to the exact size of the mount board. When using hardboard, mount the fabric against the rough side.

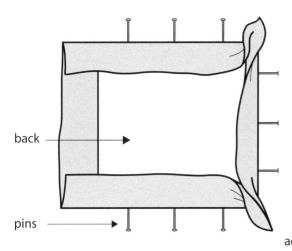

back

pins

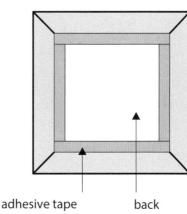

adhesive tape   back

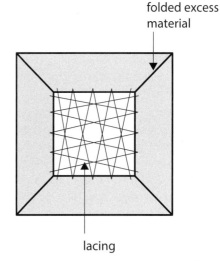

folded excess material

lacing

1 Lay the piece face down and place the mount board on top with the wadding [batting] in between. Fold the fabric up and pin to the edges of the board. Turn and check for positioning (you may need to re-pin a few times). Ensure the edges of the board align with the weave of the fabric.

2 Hardboard will not take pins so use adhesive tape for positioning. If you don't want any lacing, fold the corners neatly, pull the fabric taut and tape the fabric fold-over to the back of the board all round. Be aware that any adhesive tape eventually deteriorates; never use on or near the embroidered area.

3 Fold the fabric corners neatly and start lacing across the back from the middle of one of the shorter sides. Use a strong thread and work a giant herringbone stitch (p. 26) from side to side to avoid straining on a single hole in the fabric. Keep the thread tight enough to pull the surface taut without distorting the embroidery. Repeat across the two remaining sides.

GLOSSARY

Aari a small hooked awl used in Indian embroidery, similar to the western tambour hook

Aida block weave foundation fabric with regular construction and visible stitch holes

Appliqué decoration cut from one piece of fabric and stitched to another

Assisi thirteenth-century embroidery technique from the Italian town of the same name

Basting *see Tacking*

Batting *see Wadding*

Bias lies along any diagonal line between the lengthwise and crosswise grains

Blackwork sixteenth-century embroidery worked in black thread on white linen

Blending filament fine metallic thread for combining with ordinary stranded cotton

Blocking stretching and pinning a fabric to shape

Border decorative frame stitched around a design

Chart grid-type guide to stitch placement in counted-thread embroidery

Couching a thick thread or group of threads sewn down with a thinner thread

Count number of threads per 2.5 cm [1 in] in a foundation fabric

Crewel work Wool embroidery on linen, popular for furnishings in the seventeenth century

Digitize conversion of an image to a format that the embroidery machine can interpret

Evenweave foundation fabric with the same number of threads per 2.5 cm [1 in] counted vertically and horizontally

Filling series of stitches used to cover the area within an outline

Finishing trimming threads, removing excess backing, pressing and so on after embroidery is complete

Florentine style counted thread embroidery worked vertically in straight stitch

Frame a four-sided structure that holds fabric taut during embroidery

Freestyle embroidery hand embroidery stitches not linked with the counted-thread technique

Free motion (free machine) technique of machine stitching with free movement of fabric and stabilizer secured in a hoop

Grain the direction in which the warp and weft threads of a fabric lie

Hoop (tambour) consists of an inner and outer ring of wood or plastic tightened together to hold fabric taut during embroidery

Hooping technique of setting up and using an embroidery hoop for machine embroidery

Interfacing non-woven textile that adds body to fabric, either sew-in or iron-on (fusible)

Jump stitch a stitch taken to 'jump' across a join or from one part of a design to another

Lark's head knot (loop start) technique for securing thread at the start of work

Monogram embroidered initials

Motif a distinctive design element

Perforated paper lightweight card with regularly spaced holes imitating embroidery canvas

Perle (pearl) shiny twisted embroidery thread, non-divisible

Powdering a single stitch repeated at random across the surface of the fabric

RS the right side or 'face' of the fabric

Sampler a decorative display of a variety of embroidery stitches

Scaling proportional enlargement or reduction of a design

Seam allowance distance between the cut edge of the fabric and the seam line

Selvedge [selvage] the solid edge of a woven textile

Space-dyed threads factory-dyed in multiple colours, or in shades of a single colour at regular intervals

Stabilizer helps prevent fabric from shifting or stretching during stitching

Stay stitching a line of straight stitches to prevent a curved edge stretching out of shape

Stranded divisible embroidery cotton [floss]

Tacking preliminary stitching, removed when work is finished

Tambour *see Hoop*

Tweeding Working with different-coloured strands in the same needle.

Variegated *see Space-dyed*

Vilene *see Interfacing*

WS the wrong side of the fabric

Wadding filling material used as insulation or to pad mounted fabric

Warp threads running lengthwise in a woven fabric, parallel to the selvedge [selvage]

Waste knot starting knot placed on RS of fabric and later cut off

Weft threads running crosswise in a woven fabric, at right-angles to the selvedge [selvage]

Z-twist threads spun clockwise

INDEX OF STITCHES

QUILTING AND APPLIQUÉ

Quilting is the process of using a simple running stitch to sew together the three layers of any quilted article, from a brooch to a bed quilt. These three layers – called the quilt 'sandwich' – consist of a top fabric (which might be patchwork); a middle layer of wadding [batting]; and a lining fabric. Plain or patterned fabrics lend themselves to quilting so it isn't necessary to have patchwork as your top fabric.

Quilting is both a functional and decorative means of holding the quilt filling in place. It is ideally suited to the beginner, who can opt either to create a few simple lines or a more complicated design, such as an ornate shell or perhaps a leaf shape. By hand or machine, the quilting of the three layers will give it an eye-catching, three-dimensional quality.

Appliqué consists of sewing a cut-out fabric motif onto a background material, which may be quilted too. The reader is shown various methods and techniques in easy, illustrated stages. The terminology used throughout is UK-standard, but we have included relevant US terms in square brackets [ ] to make this a practical guide for all readers.

Fabric quilting is thought to go back as far as Ancient Egypt, but relatively recent examples exist from the early Middle Ages, including padded undergarments worn by knights to make their armour more comfortable. And for several centuries in Europe, quilted petticoats, sleeves, doublets and waistcoats provided much-needed insulation during harsh weather.

Although people associate quilting with bed covers, other items can be enhanced, such as cases for needles, spectacles or mobile phones, and soft furnishings like cushions or table runners. However, bed quilts were the main focus of quilters in the eighteenth and nineteenth centuries; warm bedding being essential in the days before central heating.

While uniformly quilted 'whole cloth' bed covers were popular in the United Kingdom, a different tradition evolved in the early United States. There, quilt tops were sewn from smaller individual pieces into blocks in a huge variety of patterns. These were more convenient to sew than large pieces, especially when travelling by wagon train. A large part of a bride's dowry were the quilts she'd accumulated, especially in the days before manufactured blankets and in areas where wool was rare. Young women often made quilt tops to be stashed away in a chest until her engagement was announced. Then family and friends gathered at 'quilting bees', so the quilts would be completed by the wedding day.

There are many ways to quilt a piece of work, dependent on the time you can devote to it, or the effect you wish to achieve. Some types – such as sashiko from Japan and kantha from India – involve stitching together just two layers, omitting the filling. Machine quilting, using a quilting foot, is quicker but hand-quilting is undoubtedly more relaxing.

Beginners need not worry about the number of hand stitches per inch but aim initially for their stitches to be spaced evenly and of equal length. Fortunately there are neither patchwork nor quilting police! It is better to join the three layers together – whether tufted [tied] at intervals, or stitched in a pattern – so that your work will be completed rather than remain as a UFO (Unfinished Object). Perfecting your quilting style will come naturally with practice and give you the confidence to try larger pieces.

PART ONE

EQUIPMENT AND MATERIALS

USING A ROTARY CUTTER

How to position the acrylic ruler and rotary cutter when cutting shapes.

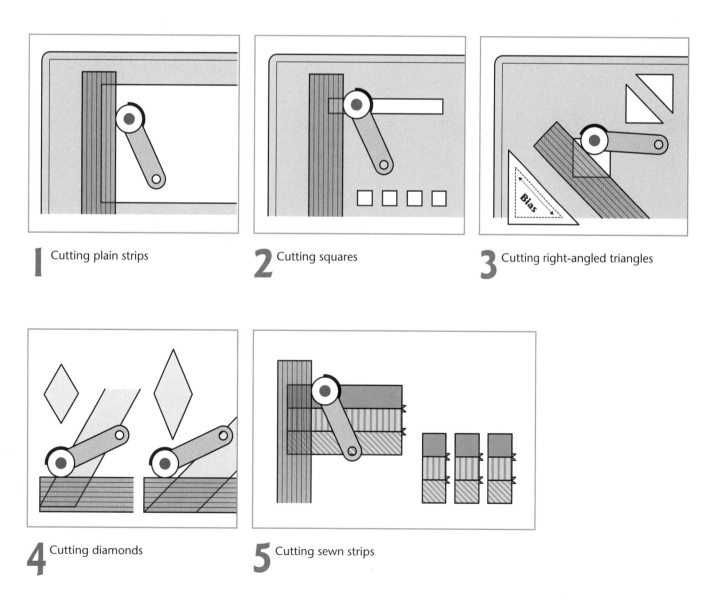

1 Cutting plain strips

2 Cutting squares

3 Cutting right-angled triangles

4 Cutting diamonds

5 Cutting sewn strips

BASIC EQUIPMENT

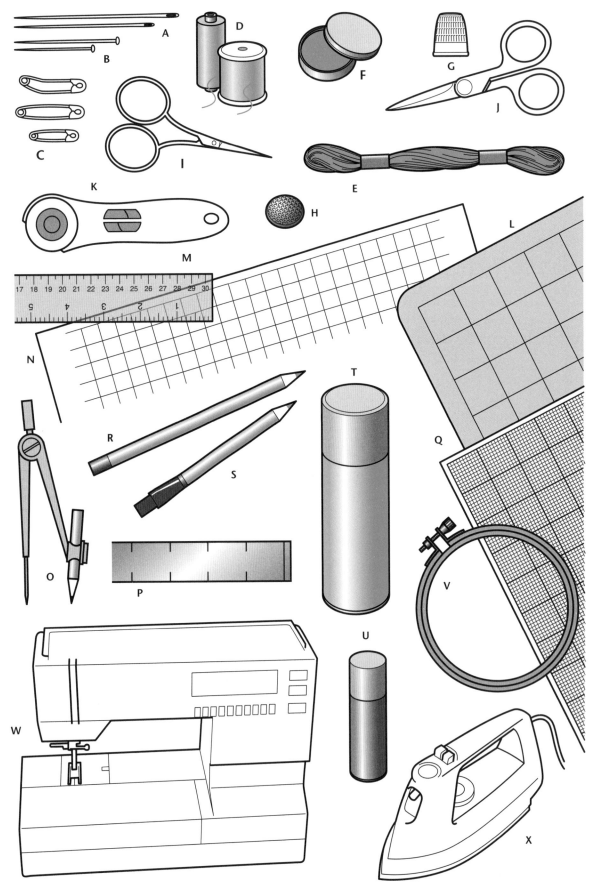

A

B

C

D

F

G

J

I

K

E

H

L

M

N

Q

R

S

T

O

P

V

U

W

X

A 'Between' needles for hand quilting (sizes 8–10 are average) and crewel (embroidery) needles for kantha and sashiko

B Pins for tacking [basting] and appliqué

C Safety pins for tacking [basting] quilt layers; curved ones can be easier to handle

D Cotton thread for machine sewing; cotton and/or hand quilting thread (heavier weight) for hand quilting

E Cotton embroidery thread for sashiko, kantha and tied quilting

F Beeswax, useful when using ordinary cotton or synthetic thread for hand quilting. Drawing the thread across the wax makes it less prone to tangle

G Thimble

H Small metal or leather stick-on pads help to prevent hand-quilter's callous

I Embroidery scissors for cutting thread and appliqué shapes

J Craft scissors for cutting templates

K Rotary cutter, capable of cutting through wadding [batting] and up to 6 layers of cotton patchwork fabric. A locking mechanism retracts the blade for safety. Use in conjunction with a cutting mat (**L**), clear ruler (**M**) and quilter's acrylic ruler (**N**), available in different lengths and widths, with a range of markings

O Compass and metal ruler (**P**) – useful for constructing templates that can be made from recycled plastic or cardboard packaging. Use in conjunction with graph paper (**Q**)

R Quilter's fabric-marking pen for marking quilt lines or drawing around appliqué shapes on fabric

S Chalk pencil with a brush at the end

T Spray adhesive for basting quilt layers together

U Repositionable glue stick for positioning appliqué shapes onto fabric or template material before cutting around them

V Hoop for holding layers to be hand quilted

W Sewing machine

X Iron

FABRIC

Modern fabrics consist of natural or man-made fibres, often mixed to combine their best qualities. Every woven fabric belongs to one of three types.

Woven fabric

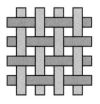

1 Plain weave Alternate warp (lengthwise) threads go over one and under one of the weft (crosswise) threads. Linen, poplin, muslin and organza are familiar examples.

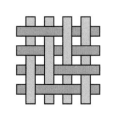

2 Twill weave Interlaces warp and weft threads over and under two or more threads progressively, to produce a clear diagonal pattern on hardwearing fabrics like denim or gabardine.

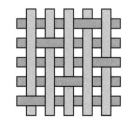

3 Satin weave A smooth, glossy, compact surface created by long silky 'floats' that leave no weft visible; the reverse is matt.

Shrinkage

The tighter the weave, the less likely a fabric is to shrink during or after manufacture. The shop label will say if a fabric is pre-shrunk. If not, and if necessary, shrink it yourself before use. Wash and dry according to the care label; this will also reveal whether the fabric is colourfast.

The grain

The grain of a fabric is the direction in which the warp and weft threads lie. The warp runs lengthwise, parallel to the selvedge [selvage]; this is the *lengthwise grain*. The weft follows the *crosswise grain*, at right angles to the selvedge [selvage].

The bias

The bias lies along any diagonal line between the lengthwise and crosswise grains. True bias is at the 45-degree angle, where you will get the maximum stretch. Bias strips are often used for piping and binding edges because of their flexibility on curves and corners.

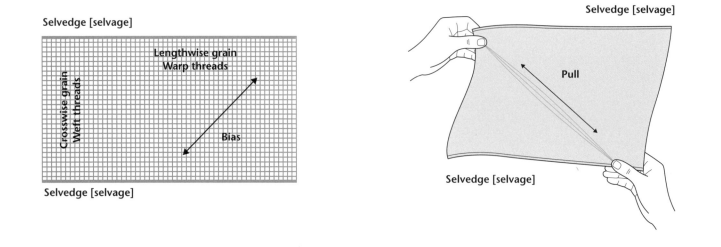

Wadding [batting]

Wadding [batting] forms the central layer of a quilted project. It can be made from natural fibres (cotton, wool, alpaca, silk or bamboo); synthetic (polyester); or a combination of these. It is sold by the metre or yard in various widths and colours. Some filling fibres are more suited to machine-washing while others respond better to hand-washing (always follow the manufacturer's advice). It's clearly preferable to use a machine-washable one for a child's quilt.

Weight and thickness 60g [2 oz] is generally the thinnest, followed by 115g, 180g and 220g [4 oz, 6 oz and 8 oz]. One is available weighing less than 60g [2 oz], which enables the hand quilter to work more stitches to the centimetre [inch].

Shrinkage Synthetic waddings [battings] shrink very little, if at all. They are good for hand quilting and tying. Natural fibres do suffer shrinkage, which can be minimized before quilting, although some prefer the crinkled look of their quilt once it has shrunk. Do observe the manufacturer's advice on this.

Which type of wadding [batting]? Black is available in 100 per cent polyester or a cotton/polyester blend, for quilts made of dark fabrics. For quilting light fabrics, cotton is available in natural (cream) or unbleached. Wool, silk, alpaca and bamboo are also usually unbleached. Polyester is available in white. Some natural cotton batting may have seed heads left in it, which may show through the top of a light-coloured quilt.

Expense Polyester wadding [batting] is the least expensive, but beware – some cheap products can 'beard', which means the act of stitching pulls fibres through to the top. This gets worse if you try to pull the fibres out. In general, cotton and natural fillings 'beard' less than synthetic. It is worth buying from a reputable quilt shop to obtain a quality wadding [batting] that 'needles' well.

How much to use? For large projects, buy a total of 30 cm [12 in] beyond the length and width of your finished quilt top; for medium-sized projects, a total of 20 cm [8 in] more; and for smaller projects, 10 cm [4 in]. Allow extra wadding [batting] for the quilt hoop or frame to grip so that you can quilt up to the edge of your project.

> **Polyester wadding [batting] can arrive badly creased through packaging. Spread it out flat and use a hair dryer to relax and remove the creases.**

> **Never use synthetic wadding [batting] in an oven mitt or potholder – too much heat can cause it to melt. Cotton towelling is a more suitable alternative.**

Fat quarters

A 'fat quarter' means getting larger pieces of fabric than are possible from a standard quarter of a yard, including strips twice as long on the lengthwise grain (see figure). The metric system in Europe may not always cater for fat quarters from retailers, but they are readily available online.

This can bring increased variety to your fabric 'stash' because they are sold both individually and in sets or 'bunches', in co-ordinated or even contrasting colourways, and also in plains and prints. This means you can buy smaller quantities of fabric that will enhance each other. Whole quilts can be made from fat quarters.

Crosswise grain

Selvedge [selvage]
lengthwise grain

Fat quarter
18 x 22 in

Fat eighth
11 x 18 in

Selvedge [selvage]

One yard of fabric, 36 x 44 in

Regular quarter yard, 9 x 44 in

Calculating quantities

The standard widths for fabric are: 90, 115 and 150 cm [36, 44–45 and 54 in]. Dress-weight fabric is usually 115 cm [44–45 in]; muslin and interfacings come in 90 cm [36 in] widths.

Study your pattern. How many different templates does it use? How many patches of each shape? Before calculating, take 5 cm [2 in] off the width for shrinkage and removal of selvedges [selvages]. *Be sure to include seam allowances.*

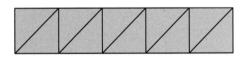

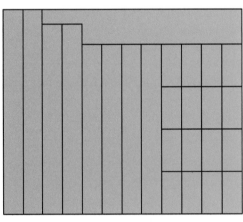

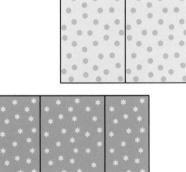

1 See how many times a template fits into the fabric width, then divide that number into the total of patches required in that particular shape.

2 Do the same for the number of lengthwise strips for borders and sashing (pp. 90 and 95).

3 Be prepared to piece together two or three widths for lining, according to the quilt size.

To estimate the length of fabric needed after 1 and 2, divide the total number of patches by the number in a single width and multiply the result by the width of the template.

An economical cutting plan takes straight strips from one edge of the fabric and irregular shapes from the other. Bias-binding or piping around the edges uses strips cut on the diagonal, which will lead to some wastage.

THE SEWING MACHINE

A well-built sewing machine will give decades of service if it is properly used and maintained.

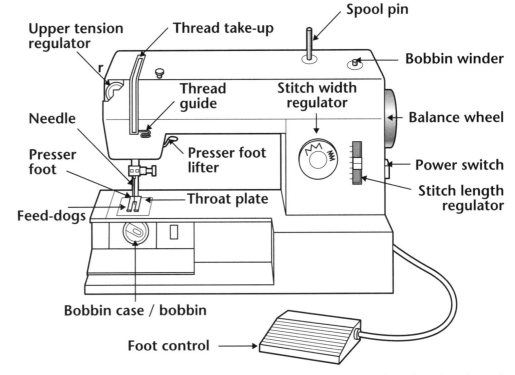

Regularly clear fluff [lint] from the feed-dogs and bobbin area. Oil the machine according to the maker's instructions. Avoid bent needles by raising the needle high before removing work and don't drag on it while stitching. Always raise the presser foot while threading the machine and lower it when you put the machine away. *Switch the power off before disconnecting plugs, cleaning or attempting repairs.*

Newer-style machines incorporate tension discs, thread guides and take-up lever inside their casings, avoiding various steps involved with threading older models. Note that some needles thread from front to back and some from left to right. Incorrect threading is probably responsible for more beginners' problems than anything else. If you have no printed instructions, search for your make and model on the web, where a huge range of manuals are available.

Four machine feet that can form a basic kit for quilters (see also p. 91):

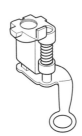

1 **Straight-stitch** The general-purpose presser foot supplied on every machine.

2 **Zigzag** Has a horizontal slot to allow for the 'swing' of the needle as it forms a zigzag with the thread.

With multiple needles (p.91) use this foot for straight stitching *only*.

3 **Darning/embroidery** Used in free motion stitching together with lowered feed-dogs and hooped fabric, this sprung foot allows manoeuvrability of fabric and close control of stitching while protecting the fingers.

4 **Walking/quilting** Uses teeth to feed upper and lower layers of fabric together evenly and avoid bunching.

QUILTING FRAMES AND HOOPS

Hoops and frames come in a range of sizes and may be held in the lap or clamped to a table. Some are floor-standing and have fully adjustable tilt for ease of use. (see p.15)

For the hand quilter, a frame or hoop is extremely useful because it ensures all three layers are held taut and wrinkle-free, thus reducing the likelihood of any stitches catching a wrinkle on the underside. The three layers still need to be tacked [basted] with needle and thread or safety pins. An adhesive tacking spray may be used instead.

Once the quilt layers are clamped in a frame, they should be fairly taut but not so tight that the fabric is distorted.

The traditional wooden roller-frame is floor-standing, providing a rectangular quilting surface, with two rollers the width of the quilt and two stretchers that keep the layers taut by holding the rollers in place. However, it is extremely heavy and takes up a lot of space.

'Lap quilting' without a frame is possible provided that all layers are thoroughly tacked [basted] to prevent them shifting while being handled. This useful combination of cutting mat with ironing surface on the reverse can also double as a lap support.

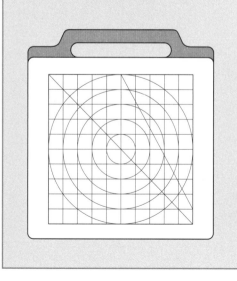

A handy alternative is the PVC frame, constructed from plastic tube resembling plumbers' piping. It provides a large rectangular surface that any size of quilt can be draped over and hand quilted. The quilt layers are held taut by clamping more 'piping' over the frame's perimeters. The advantage is that it assembles and disassembles easily; the lengths of piping are lightweight, can be stored together in a bag between projects, and carried anywhere.

In order to work to the very edge of your quilt, tack [baste] additional strips of fabric to the sides of it, and use extra wadding [batting] so the hoop or frame has something to grip. This ensures that the main quilting area remains within the frame's perimeters and not so near the edge that it becomes impossible to quilt. This technique is also useful if you are quilting a project much smaller than your frame or hoop. Remember to check the underside of your quilt frequently to ensure a wrinkle hasn't appeared.

When not quilting for a period of time, such as overnight, it is important to remove your quilt from the frame or at least substantially loosen it. If left clamped in a frame for too long, the layers will become overstretched and go baggy.

PART TWO:
QUILTING METHODS AND TECHNIQUES

QUILTING BY HAND AND MACHINE

This section covers both hand and machine quilting methods and techniques, as well as the different effects possible with quilting.

First it is important to consider whether your project and the time you have available lends itself to hand quilting or machine quilting. Indeed, both methods can be used on the same piece of work. It is also a matter of personal preference; some prefer the 'rhythm' of hand quilting and find it calming, while others feel more at home quilting with their sewing machine.

Machine quilting is quicker on larger projects such as bed quilts. It is also preferable for quilts that will need frequent washing, such as those for children or pets. However, unlike hand quilting, it means you are tied to the room where your sewing machine is, and it is tempting to spend so long machine quilting that you may find yourself suffering from shoulder or neck ache; do take frequent breaks to stretch both arms and legs. It can also prove difficult to move a large quilt through a machine in order to stitch in a different direction.

Hand quilting a large project will take longer but lends itself to quilting in different directions as it is easier to shift a quilt over a frame or hoop than through a machine. Hand quilting is more portable as the frame can be moved from room to room, taking advantage of natural daylight, and more readily taken on holiday. A combination of machine and hand quilting is a good idea where practical. For example, you could machine-quilt between your quilt blocks and along any sashing or borders, but hand quilt motifs in the spaces in between.

Many seasoned quilters prefer to use cotton thread for both hand and machine work because synthetic threads can, over time, wear through natural fibres, thus weakening quilt stitches and causing seams to separate.

If synthetic threads are used at the 'piecing' stage (sewing shapes together to form a block) or when creating appliqué, care must be taken not to use a very hot iron, in case the heat weakens the thread so the stitches fail to hold.

THE QUILT SANDWICH

Inserting wadding [batting]

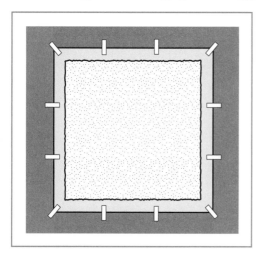

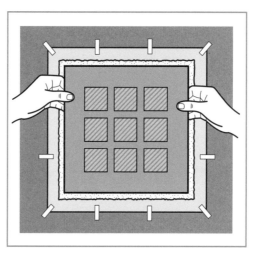

1 Press any seams in a pieced lining (p. 68). WS up, tape it to a flat surface. Centre wadding [batting] with a margin all round.

2 Having pressed the quilt top quite flat and made sure it is square, place RS up over the wadding [batting].

Pinning and tacking [basting] layers

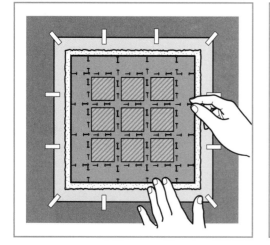

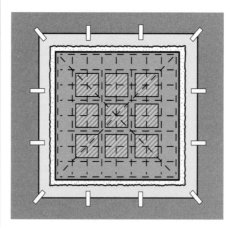

3 Pin all three layers together with long straight pins or large safety pins. You will need plenty for this stage. Alternatively, use a spray-on basting adhesive, following the manufacturer's instructions.

4 Knot the thread end and, starting at the centre, tack [baste] out towards the edges. First, stitch horizontally and vertically at 10 cm [4 in] intervals; then from the centre diagonally to each corner.

Some materials can be recycled for use as wadding [batting], such as a thin blanket or a flannel/ brushed cotton sheet. Even a plain cotton sheet can be incorporated in a lightweight summer quilt.

Starting hand quilting

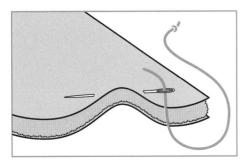 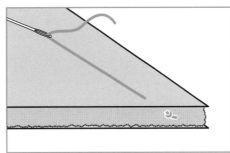 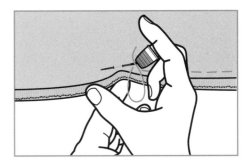

1 Thread a size 8 or 10 'between' needle with thread 30–45 cm [12–18 in] long. Tie a knot in the end. Needle in and out through both top and wadding [batting].

2 Pull the thread taut so the knot passes through the fabric to become anchored in the wadding [batting]. For a firmer hold, tie a double knot.

3 With a thimble, push the needle in at an angle until the finger beneath feels the point through all the layers. The finger below guides the needle back to the surface.

Finishing hand quilting

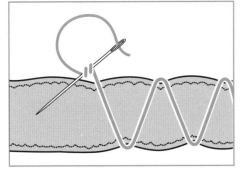 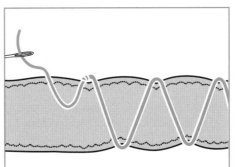 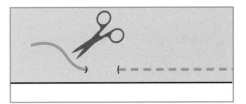

1 Tie a knot close to the quilt's surface, or wind the thread a couple of times round the needle and insert through the top and wadding [batting] where the final stitch would be.

2 Run the needle through the wadding [batting] 2.5 cm [1 in] away from the stitching line. Pull the thread taut so the knot passes through the fabric.

3 Pull the needle and thread gently to the surface and snip the thread close. Pull the fabric until the snipped end disappears below the surface.

Stitching method

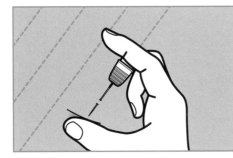 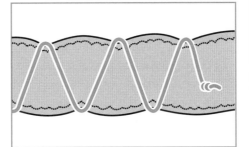 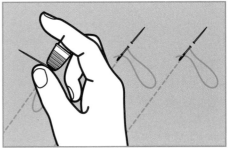

1 Following markings, stitch rows of small, even running stitches through all three layers. Rows no more than 5 cm [2 in] apart ensure the filling stays in place.

2 Stitches will get smaller with practice. Few people achieve the ideal of ten stitches per 2.5 cm [1 in] – six is more realistic. Pull the thread taut enough to make indentations in both surfaces.

3 To help work evenly across a large quilt, try having several needles threaded up at once.

Machine quilting

For quilts too thick to hand-stitch: load the machine with No. 40 cotton and a new 90/14 needle; set the stitch length to ten per 2.5 cm [1 in]. Choose a top thread that blends with your patchwork and wind two bobbins with a colour to match the lining. *Do not use any glazed hand quilting thread,* since the special wax interferes with the tension discs.

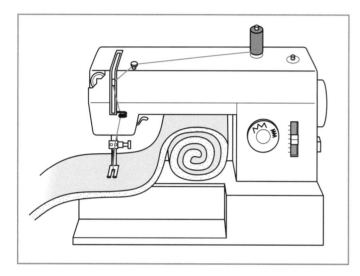

1 Roll the quilt tightly at one end and tuck under the machine throat. You can secure the rolls with bicycle clips. Begin parallel lines of stitching at the halfway point along one edge. Start and finish each line with forward and reverse stitches.

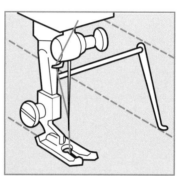

2 If you have one, use a walking/ quilting foot (p. 69). A spacer guide usefully sets a regular interval between stitch lines.

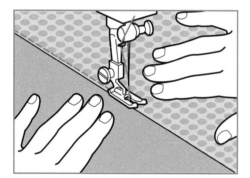

3 Don't drag the quilt as you sew as this causes skipped stitches. Smooth the fabric either side of the needle and go at a steady speed. Check the back for loops or puckers at the end of each line.

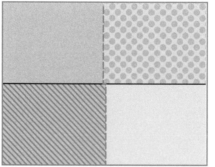

4 Ideally, seams should match but you can 'jump' a small difference across a join when stitching 'in the ditch' (see opposite).

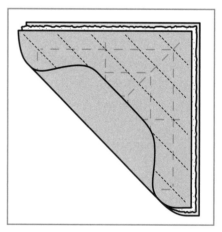

5 Roll the quilt diagonally if sewing diagonal lines. Begin at the halfway point as in Step 1.

In the ditch

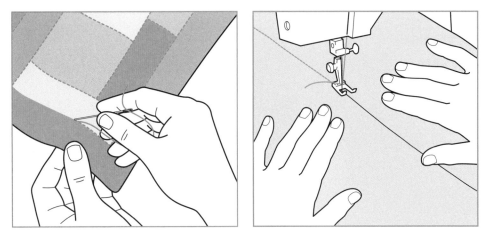

'In the ditch' describes quilting stitches in the centre of the seam. It can be done by hand (left) or machine (right) and is useful if you want your project to look quilted but would rather not use elaborately quilted motifs. When you are quilting by machine, the needle can reach the 'ditch' area more easily if you use your hands to spread open the seams and employ the walking quilting foot (p. 69). Work with an unobtrusive thread colour such as a medium grey or brown, rather than a contrasting shade.

Tied quilting

Tied [tufted] quilting is a quick method of holding layers together, although they should still be tacked [basted] beforehand. Try two colours of knitting yarn knotted together, use bright embroidery silks [floss], or even incorporate buttons *(see rear cover)*.

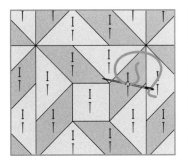
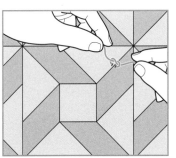
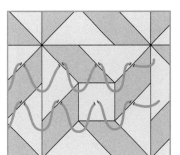
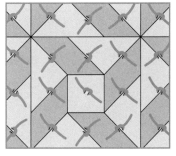

1 Mark tie [tuft] positions with long pins. Single back-stitch around each pin and cut the thread.

2 Tie the free ends in a double knot and trim level.

3 Alternatively, link all the back stitches with generous loops.

4 Cut the loops and knot each pair of ends over the central stitch.

ECHO QUILTING

Echo and contour quilting are similar in that the lines of quilting echo the shape of each appliquéd shape or patchwork piece. For example, if an appliqué features shell or petal shapes, you can add interest by quilting two or more equidistant lines around each one.

Hawaiian appliqué

In this formalized style of appliqué, intricate designs are cut from folded paper and transferred to a plain coloured fabric. The fabric is cut out and sewn onto a white background. Quilting afterwards outlines the pattern in multiple rows known as *kapa lau*.

CONTOUR QUILTING

Contour quilting emphasizes the geometric shapes in a patchworked block. Either by hand or machine, sew the decorative stitch lines approximately 7 mm [¼ in] from the seam lines. This technique is also known as 'outline stitching'.

Echo and contour quilting can be combined in the same project.

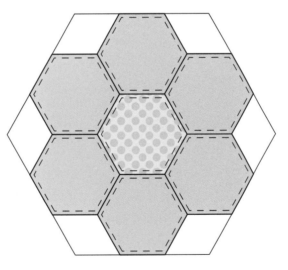

FILLING PATTERNS

Filling patterns are used to quilt large background spaces around individual motifs, or they may be used on their own to quilt an entire project. These overall patterns are an excellent treatment for larger areas, not only for the decorative effect but also to ensure that the wadding [batting] layer doesn't bunch up.

Straight-line patterns are the quickest. Attach a spacer foot (p. 74) that enables you to stitch parallel lines without having to mark them. Otherwise, use an acrylic ruler and marking pencil to draw quilting lines at regular intervals on your quilt top. The directions on your wadding [batting] packaging will indicate how far apart the quilting lines can be.

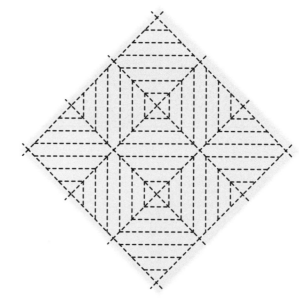

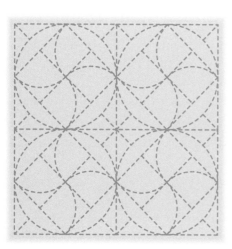

If you want a wavy filler pattern, consider using a circular or oval platter or tray as a template. Place it on your quilt top and draw along one edge, reversing the edge as you go along.

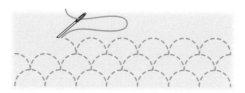

FREE MOTION QUILTING

Free motion quilting (also known as free machine quilting) provides an even quicker filling stitch because it isn't marked out first on the top fabric layer. It functions either as background or as the primary quilting pattern. The traditional wooden hoop (p. 70) can also be used with free motion work; in this case the rim is turned uppermost so that the WS of the fabric rests flat against the base plate.

Free motion is performed with a darning or embroidery foot and the machine's feed-dogs lowered or covered with a special plate. Your sewing machine manual will show how to operate the drop feed mechanism, usually via a simple lever. It is an added advantage to use a sprung foot (p. 69) because the vertical spring action prevents the top fabric coming up with the needle each time and lifting away from the wadding [batting] inside.

Because the tiny metal teeth of the feed-dogs aren't engaged below and you have set your stitch length dial to zero, you are free to move the quilt in any direction through the machine. You will need practice to coordinate the stitch speed and movement of the fabric. It is important to run the machine at a constant speed in order to maintain a consistent stitch length. The general rule is to stitch fast but move the fabric slowly. Use a thread near the colour of the top layer if you want the quilting to blend in.

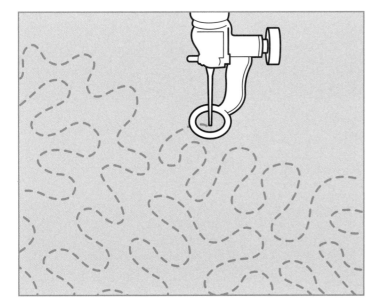

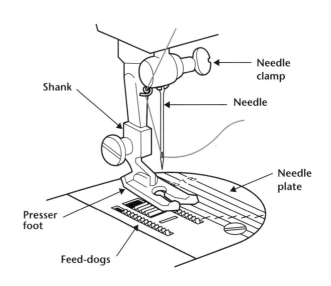

Needle clamp

Shank

Needle

Needle plate

Presser foot

Feed-dogs

KANTHA

Kantha (meaning 'rags') is a traditional hand stitching technique from Bangladesh, on the Indian subcontinent, sewn predominantly with a running stitch and usually in different colour threads.

It is worked through multiple layers of fine cotton fabric without wadding [batting], though you could use a very thin filling material. Thick wadding [batting] would make the stitches too difficult to pull through.

Kantha uses both stylized motifs and pictorial design. Coloured threads are used to stitch the outline of a motif or figure, such as the bird shown here. Then the inside is filled with consecutive stitch lines in various complementary colours. The background is stitched in a thread that matches the colour of the background fabric.

As with sashiko (opposite), the kantha stitch method is to pleat the fabric onto the tip of the needle and make as many stitches as possible before pulling the needle through and smoothing out the fabric.

Kantha threads Use a single strand of cotton embroidery thread such as perle [pearl] or two or three strands of floss.

Fabric Choose soft fabrics such as lawn or muslin, which allow ease of stitching. In Bangladesh, recycled sari fabrics were traditionally used in kantha work.

Needle Use a sashiko needle, or a large 'sharp' or crewel needle. The eye must be big enough to accommodate thicker strands.

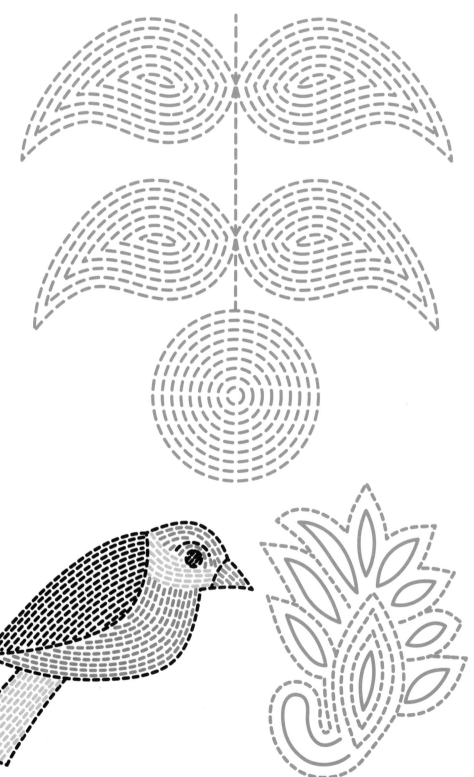

SASHIKO

This Japanese style of running-stitch embroidery is not usually quilted directly through wadding [batting] but worked through one or two layers of fabric and then backed by a layer of filling and a lining fabric.

Around three centuries ago, Japanese working men and warriors wore indigo-dyed jackets constructed from two layers of hemp or cotton fabric and the women stitched these layers together for durability. They traditionally used white thread on a dark blue background and sashiko needles 5 cm [2 in] long with a uniform shaft. The stitch pattern for everyday wear was fairly plain but they developed elaborate designs for special occasions.

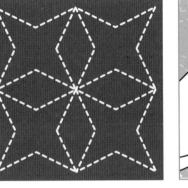
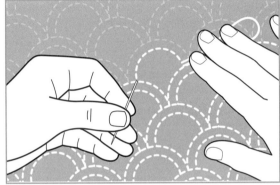

Threads Specialist sashiko threads are generally used double; alternatives are stranded embroidery cotton [floss] or a shiny perle [pearl] twist. The stitches may be longer than for regular quilting – sashiko uses a long running stitch at five or six stitches to 2.5 cm [1 in] – but aim to keep them all the same length.

Use your cutting mat, acrylic ruler and marking pencil to draw a grid on a piece of sashiko fabric. Stitch lines can then be devised or you could use a cardboard template to create the curved lines of the shell pattern, for example. Horizontal and vertical lines are usually stitched first and then the diagonals. Any other shapes are done last.

Fabric Sashiko fabrics have a lower thread count than ordinary cottons, which enables the thread to be pulled through more easily. However, normal cotton patchwork fabrics can be combined with a single thread for the stitching.

Needle As with those for kantha work, a long needle with a large eye is necessary for the thicker threads, for example a large 'sharp' or a crewel embroidery needle.

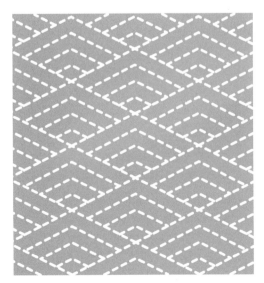

CORDED QUILTING

Sometimes known as Italian quilting, this technique embellishes solid-coloured fabrics with a raised design. It has no internal layer of wadding [batting].

The corded effect is achieved by sewing twin lines of running stitch through two layers of fabric and then (from the WS) inserting lengths of cord between both the layers and the two lines of stitching.

Apart from a straightforward stripe or lattice design, you might begin with a simple spiral, leaf shape or initial letter. Place a sheet of heavy tracing paper or plastic (Kodatrace) over the original image and trace it. Create a template by cutting out the traced shape.

Position the template on the surface of the fabric and draw a double line round it with a fabric marker pen. Take care to keep the channel between the lines the correct width throughout the design; too narrow, and the cord will not fit; too wide and the cord will barely show as raised.

Fabrics Use a close-woven plain coloured cotton for the top and a looser weave for the backing. The latter makes it easier to enter the stitched channel with the threader. Cut both bits of fabric the same size, including a seam allowance if necessary.

Cord Use pre-shrunk piping cord or candlewick (a thick, soft cotton embroidery thread). Synthetic knitting yarn can also be used.

Needle A bodkin or blunt-tipped needle will serve as a threader, so long as the eye can take the cord, and the tip doesn't pierce the fabric in the wrong places. Insert the cord through a loop of ordinary thread and pull both through the eye of the threader.

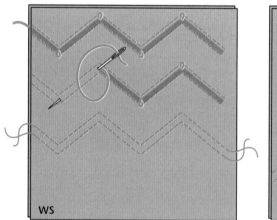

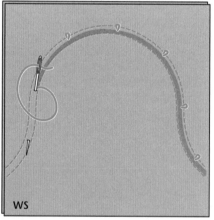

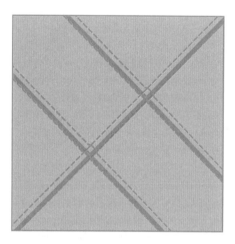

Insert the threader tip into the WS and guide it through the stitched channel, pulling very gently. Where lines cross or bend sharply, the needle and cord are brought out and reinserted, leaving a small loop at the back of the fabric to 'ease' and avoid puckering. When complete, leave a short tail of cord (1 cm [½ in]) at the back of the work, not a knot.

Avoid stitching across channels at intersections by using a 'jump' stitch on each line (p. 74). If channels are blocked, don't cut the stitching or it will come undone too far. Instead, bring out the cord on the WS on both lines and cross them over before reinserting.

TRAPUNTO

Trapunto is Italian for 'embroider'. This centuries-old technique is also known as 'stuffed quilting', where motifs are padded so that they appear in relief against the background fabric. The raised motifs can be enhanced further by hand or machine stitching a filling pattern over the background area.

Fabric A plain glazed cotton will show up the motifs better than a matt fabric. Alternatively, if you have a themed fabric, featuring shapes such as animals or fruit, you can stitch around these shapes and stuff them through a slit in the backing fabric. Sometimes the backing fabric has such a loose weave that the stuffing can be worked in through it, rather than cutting a slit.

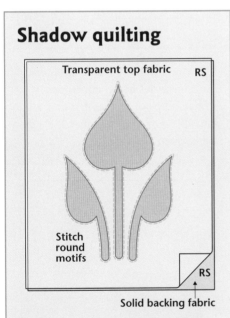

Shadow quilting

Transparent top fabric — RS

Stitch round motifs

RS

Solid backing fabric

An attractive, delicate effect can be created by sandwiching a different coloured material, pre-cut to shape, between a transparent top layer such as voile and a solid backing fabric. It is then contained by hand or machine stitching. Stencil-type motifs are ideal for this technique, which is essentially decorative.

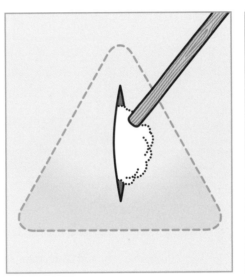

Mark out your motif on the top fabric of a quilt sandwich and then outline it with a single line of stitches through all three layers. The stuffing is inserted through a small slit in the backing fabric. This extra material can be wool, polyester filling, or whatever material is used in the rest of the work. It is best to avoid kapok or cotton wool because they form lumps too easily, especially if the item is to be washed. Use a stuffing stick or small crochet hook to push it into all areas of the motif being stuffed.

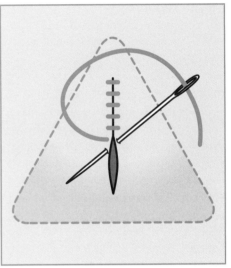

Once the areas are packed, close the slit at the back of the work. Hold the two raw edges together and oversew them with broad stitches. Finish by running the thread off into the stuffing. If the back is going to be exposed, as on a quilt, you will need to line the work afterwards.

PROJECT: COASTERS

Simple coasters are an ideal first quilting project, and would make a welcome gift.

To make 4 coasters you will need:

- Two pieces of fabric 30 x 15 cm [12 x 6 in] in two different designs for the top surfaces
- One piece of fabric 28 x 28 cm [11 x 11 in] for the backing/lining
- A piece of thin wadding [batting] 28 x 28 cm [11 x 11 in] for the filling

Make the first coaster Using an acrylic ruler and mat, cut two 8 cm [3 in] squares in two different fabrics to give four squares in total (two of each fabric). Or draw an 8 cm [3 in] square on graph paper and use as a template (this includes a 7 mm [1/4 in] seam allowance). Similarly, cut out the backing fabric and wadding directly or use graph paper to make a 14 cm [5½ in] square template.

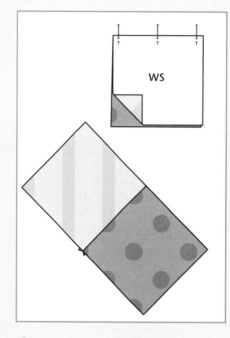

1 RS together, pin and stitch together one square of each fabric with a 7 mm [1/4 in] seam allowance to produce two pairs of squares.

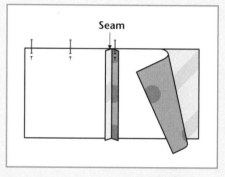

2 Ensuring that the different fabric squares fall in a chequerboard formation, place RS together, pin, and stitch the two strips together. Press the seams open.

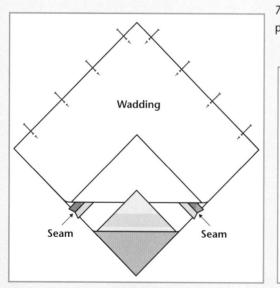

3 Place the backing and the patchwork squares RS together on the table. Put the wadding [batting] square on top of both. Pin and stitch through all three layers on all four sides, leaving an opening of 4 cm [1½ in] on one side. Snip the corners to reduce bulk and turn RS out. Oversew the opening closed.

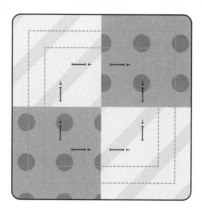

4 To quilt the coaster, machine stitch a line 7 mm [¼ in] in from the edge, marking this with pins or using the quilting foot as a guide.

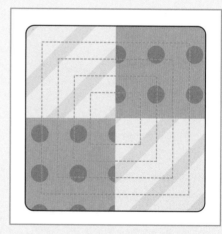

5 For further quilting, mark parallel lines in from the previous ones and finish by stitching around the perimeter.

Repeat to make a total of 4 coasters.

PART THREE:
APPLIQUÉ METHODS AND TECHNIQUES

SCALING A DESIGN

Appliqué means 'applied' and describes the technique of cutting a decorative shape from one fabric and stitching it to another, either by hand or machine. This section describes various appliqué methods.

Designs ideas can be found everywhere, however, the images we choose are seldom the precise size that we want. Here is a basic method of scaling for enlargement and reduction. Reverse the size order in Steps 2 and 3 to enlarge the image.

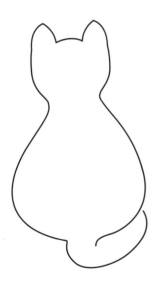

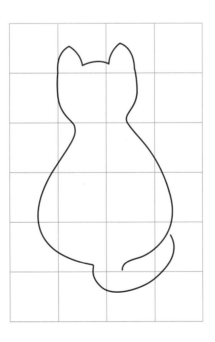

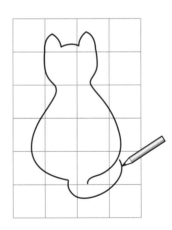

1 Trace or print out the original image.

2 Enclose outline image in a frame and divide the area into squares.

3 Rule up a smaller sheet into same number of divisions and copy the original, square by square, until the reduced design is complete and ready to form a template.

Cutting out and sewing appliqué

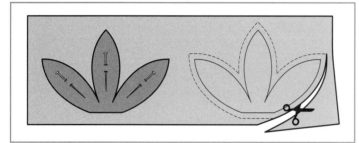

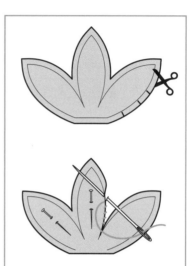

1 Pin the template to the fabric and trace round with a fabric marker. Cut out the shape with a 7 mm [¼ in] seam allowance; omit the allowance if planning to oversew (step 3).

2 Clip the curves for a smooth edge when slip-stitching the appliqué to the base fabric. With a size 8 sharps needle and waxed quilting thread, turn the seam allowance under with the needle tip as you sew.

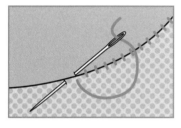

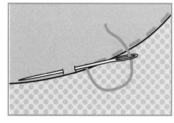

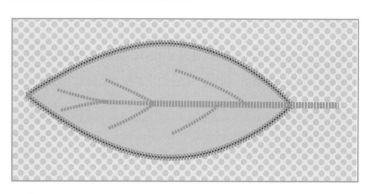

3 You can oversew the raw edges of the shape directly on to the base fabric. Stitch closely if it frays.

4 Running stitch can be used for attaching non-fraying material such as felt.

5 Appliqué by machine offers a choice of stitch effects, including zigzag and satin stitch.

Double-thickness appliqué

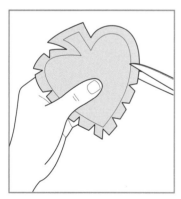

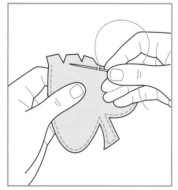

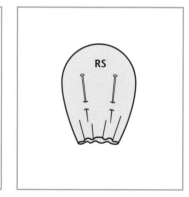

1 Pin two pieces of fabric RS together. Draw the motif on one side with a marker. Cut out with a 7mm [¼ in] seam allowance. Stitch along the drawn line, leaving a gap for turning. Clip the curves down to the stitch line.

2 Turn RS out. Smooth the seam from inside with a crochet hook. Tack [baste] around the shape, closing the gap and folding in raw edges as you go. Stitch to the base fabric all round. Remove the tacking [basting].

1 Construct a single flower petal by pinning and sewing two pieces of fabric RS together. Leave open at the base. Clip the curves before turning RS out and press if necessary.

2 Pin the layers together and stitch gathers across the base. Make five petals and attach at the base only to the background, so they appear 3D. Sew a large fabric-covered button in the centre.

USING FUSIBLE WEB

Fusible web is impregnated with heat-sensitive glue that sticks one piece of fabric to another when ironed.

It prevents the appliqué fraying and with the motif trimmed to shape, it keeps cut edges looking sharp without the need to turn them under. Some brands carry so much glue that it makes the fabric stiff and difficult to sew. Select one with a medium-strength bond.

Cut a piece of background fabric to the required size for your quilt block or project, including a 7 mm [¼ in] seam allowance. Select another fabric for the appliqué shape.

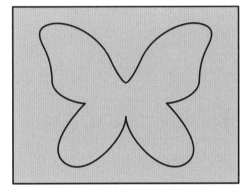

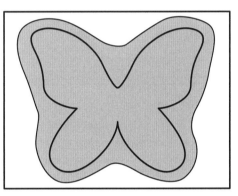

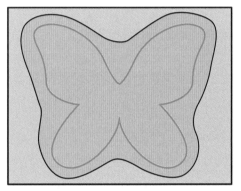

1 Draw or trace your motif onto the paper side of the fusible web. If it is an asymmetrical motif, make it a mirror image (reverse left to right).

2 With a margin of about 7 mm [¼ in], roughly cut the shape out of the fusible web.

3 Place the cut-out onto the WS of appliqué fabric, paper side uppermost, and iron to fuse the surfaces together. When cool, cut out carefully along the drawn lines.

Peel off the paper backing. There may be backing on both sides – brands vary, so do read the manufacturer's instructions. Position the prepared appliqué, RS up, on the background fabric and press again. Always use a pressing cloth to keep the glue off your iron.

Fusible web creates only a temporary bond, tending to lift and curl after washing. So it is still necessary to machine the appliquéd shape into place using satin stitch, blanket stitch or several lines of straight stitching.

USING FREEZER PAPER

Freezer paper, invented as food wrapping but now available from quilting suppliers, will adhere to fabric when ironed shiny side down. It doesn't harm the iron and is the modern equivalent of using traditional paper templates cut from newspapers or old letters.

Freezer paper templates allow for greater accuracy and make the handling of shapes much easier. Quilters' freezer paper is also the right size for photocopiers and printers, so you can create multiples of any one shape. If using printer ink, check whether it is washable, in case it marks your fabric.

Preparing the shape

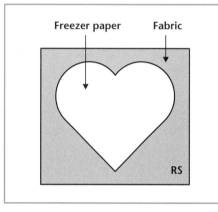

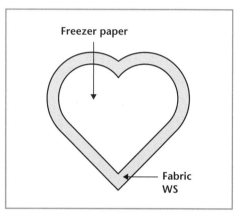

1 A heart shape is ideal for practice. Trace, draw, photocopy or print onto the matt (non-shiny) side of the freezer paper then, on an ironing board, lay the paper shiny side down onto the RS of your fabric. Press with a hot dry iron. The paper will adhere to the fabric in a few seconds. Cut out the heart shape with a margin of 7 mm [¼ in] all round and peel off the paper.

2 Place the fabric heart WS up on the board and reposition the paper, shiny side up.

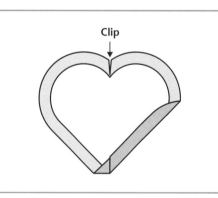

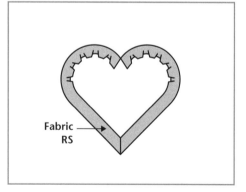

3 Press the point of the heart up with the tip or edge of the iron. Make sure it sticks to the paper.

4 Clip curves where necessary. Continue to press the fold-over margin onto the paper all around the heart.

5 If the paper lifts away, reapply the iron and hold with your fingertips until the paper cools.

Attaching the shape

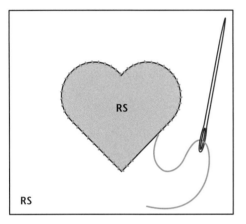

6 Pin the heart to the backing fabric, RS up. Sew with a stabbing motion, coming up through the appliquéd shape and going back down through the backing. The stitches should be quite close together. Avoid going through the freezer paper if possible, so that it can be more easily removed later. If you leave a gap of about 2.5 cm [1 in] you may be able to remove the paper from a small shape by working it out through the gap with a pair of tweezers. Finally, sew the gap shut.

Sewing by machine Use an appliqué foot (p. 91) if available, as it enables you to see where the stitches are. Set to a very small zigzag stitch, or use the machine hemstitch, which employs a sequence of several straight stitches, then a zigzag. With the hemstitch, the straight stitches should be in the background fabric only, as close as possible to the edge of the appliqué.

Removing the paper

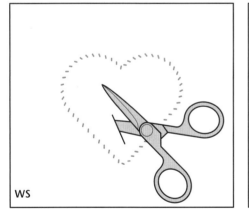

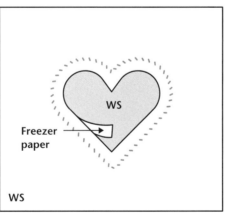

Freezer paper

7 On the WS, cut a slit in the backing fabric and gently pull the freezer paper out through the slit. Be careful not to pierce the heart shape with the tip of the scissors. There is no real need to sew up this slit since the piece will either be lined or become the top layer of a quilt sandwich where the reverse will not be seen. Finally, press very lightly.

8 For larger areas, it is best to cut away all the backing fabric that lies immediately behind the appliqué, leaving a 7 mm [¼ in] seam allowance. Again, take care not to pierce the heart shape with the scissors. Gently pull out the freezer paper, not forgetting to strip out the pieces under the seam. Finally, press very lightly.

QUILTING APPLIQUÉD BLOCKS

Just like traditional patchwork, appliquéd blocks may be sewn together to form a quilt top.

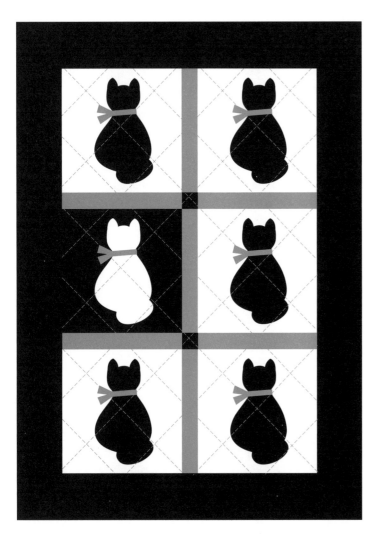

Instead of joining the blocks edge to edge, sashing (also called latticing) may be used, where narrow strips of fabric separate – and effectively frame – each motif (see illustration).

The whole quilt sandwich can then be assembled and quilted in straight lines, or by stitching around each motif, once or even several times (p. 76). If there are larger background areas not covered by appliqué, there's the possibility of using a filling pattern by the free motion machining method (p. 79).

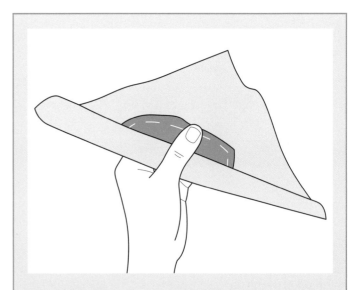

When sewing appliqué in hand, fold or roll the project in your free hand to get a good grip on the stitch area and keep your wrist straight to avoid cramp in your thumb.

MACHINING APPLIQUÉ

Machine accessories

Open toe appliqué A useful variation on the standard zigzag foot, the widely-spaced toes on this foot afford a clear view of appliqué and quilting work.

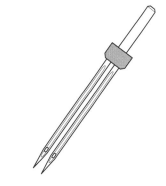

Appliqué/embroidery The toes on this foot are shorter, for smoother stitching, improved visibility and manoeuvrability.

Twin needle Requires two spools of top thread but interlocks with a single bobbin. The effect is two equidistant stitch lines on top and a zigzag beneath.

Threads

The range of synthetic machine threads includes metallics and 'invisible' monofilaments. Take care not to melt synthetics when ironing. Some perform better than others, depending on the nylon or polyester filament; ask your supplier for recommendations. If using a cotton thread, choose a neutral colour to blend with the backing fabric. However, one that contrasts with both backing and appliqué will accentuate the appliqué shape. Fine silk threads are excellent for hand sewing.

Tension

Regular machine stitching is formed by the top and lower threads interlocking in the fabric.

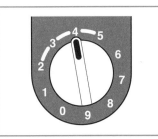

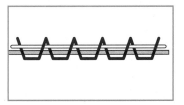

1 Top thread tension is governed by the tension dial, numbered 0–9. Behind it, the thread runs between two or three discs that are adjusted according to the dial.

2 Between 4 and 5 on the dial is considered 'normal' tension. The threads meet in the centre of the fabric and the stitching appears the same on each side.

3 Below 4, the tension discs loosen and the top thread runs more freely. The thread can then pass through both layers of fabric. This is only desirable if you want to create gathers by pulling up the bottom thread.

4 Above 5, the discs are screwed together more tightly and the reverse happens.

Most modern sewing machines produce a number of decorative embroidery stitches. Try one of these to stitch around a plain appliquéd shape.

When you have finished, leave long thread ends. Gently pull the bobbin thread on the WS, and a tiny loop of the top thread will appear. Pull this loop through to the WS and tie a knot with the bobbin thread. Now thread a needle with both threads and tidy them away with a couple of stitches into the back of the work.

PROJECT: FELT NEEDLECASE

This simple project is ideal for beginners. It makes a surprisingly durable and attractive item and a useful gift. It uses felt, which doesn't fray, so the motifs are easily cut out and appliquéd with a neat blanket stitch.

To make the felt needlecase you will need:

- Several sheets of wool-mixture felt, approx. 20 cm [8 in] square
- Flannel, felt or soft muslin for inner pages, approx. 20 cm [8 in] square
- Sewing thread for attaching pages to cover
- Stranded embroidery cotton [floss] or perle [pearl] twist for edging and appliqué
- An embroidery needle
- Trimmings such as buttons or sequins
- Sharp scissors

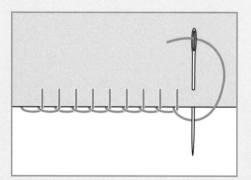

Blanket stitch Start with a knot, bring needle through to RS at stitch height and oversew fabric edge once, forming a loop. Pass needle through loop and pull tight against edge. Working from left to right, push needle into fabric again at same height. Pull needle forwards through new loop to form a half-hitch. Tighten as before. Repeat and fasten off with extra half-hitch around final loop.

Method

Cut a piece of felt, 10 x 20 cm [4 x 8 in]. Folded in half, this forms the cover of the finished case, 10 x 10 cm [4 x 4 in]. Buttonhole stitch all around the edge in a contrasting coloured thread.

On paper, trace any of the motifs from the opposite page (or devise your own). Use them as templates to outline and cut out felt shapes, which will decorate the outer cover of the case.

Arrange and tack [baste] your chosen shapes onto the outer case, then blanket stitch them into position. Use a thread that contrasts with the appliqué motif.

For the inner 'pages' – where the needles and pins go – cut one piece of felt, flannel or muslin, 8.5 x 18.5 cm [3½ x 7¼ in], and the second one smaller, 6.5 x 16.5 cm [2⅝ x 6½ in]. If you have pinking shears, prepare the pages with them to make a decorative zigzag edge and reduce fraying.

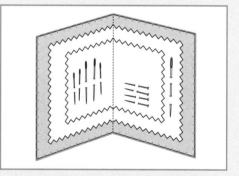

Open the cover out flat, WS up, and place the larger page on top of it with an equal margin all round. Next, place the smaller page on the larger one, again with an equal margin all round. Tack [baste] the three layers together down the centre, from top to bottom, and then machine stitch them for permanence.

Cover the stitching if you wish, with a length of narrow ribbon that matches the colour of the buttonhole edging. Tie it in a bow on the outer spine and secure with a couple of stitches through the centre bow. Add any buttons, beads, sequins and so forth to the outer cover, if required.

PROJECT IDEAS AND MOTIFS

Create a picture with fabric of a teacup, pet or house and using
novelty buttons or beads.

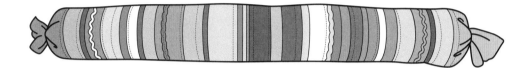

Make a draught excluder from a piece of fabric the length of a doorway and about
30 cm [12 in] wide. Sew several rows of braid, bias binding, ribbon and lace across
the width. Make casings at each end to to take drawstrings. Sew up the long side
to create a sausage shape. Thread and close one of the casings with a drawstring,
stuff with wadding, then repeat at the other end.

TRIMMINGS

Suitable trimmings include braid, ric-rac, cord, ribbon, bias binding and lace. Other embellishments include sequins, beads, buttons, shells and even dollshouse miniatures like tiny scissors.

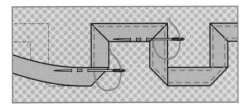

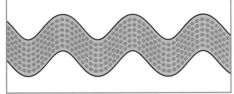

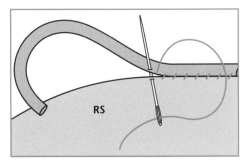

Outlining with braid Add emphasis to applied shapes by outlining them. Braid may be sewn by hand or machine so long as it is done with precision and no wrinkles.

Ric-rac braid This narrow, flexible braid woven in zigzag formation is a popular basic trimming.

Outlining in cord Cord defines curves where straight braid cannot. It is slip stitched by hand; the needle passes through the cord and picks up threads at the edge of the appliqué, pulling the two together.

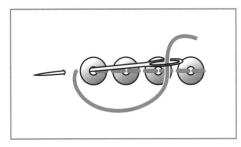

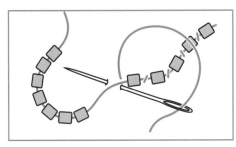

Applying sequins Secure the thread on the WS and bring the needle up through the eye of first sequin. Back stitch over the right-hand edge, come out on the left-hand edge and back stitch down through the eye. Advance a stitch and repeat with the next sequin.

Applying beads Thread up two needles and secure both threads on the WS. Bring the first needle through and thread it with a number of beads. Take the second needle and stitch across the first thread coming through the first bead. Slide the second bead close to the first and repeat until all are in place.

Check that trimmings are safe to wash. If not, they would be better suited to wall-hangings than bed covers. Fabrics such as lace and ric-rac may be pre-shrunk by a warm-water soak beforehand. Take care when pressing any synthetics. Small embellishments – even buttons – that could be pulled off or swallowed should not go on a young child's quilt, although they could be used in a wall hanging that is kept out of reach.

Project ideas

Construct a personalized greetings card, using ribbon to appliqué a friend's name or flower motif onto a small piece of fabric. Attach this to the front of a blank card.

Wider ribbons or braid can make an effective border for a project, or use several rows of the same material such as ric-rac in graduated colours, for example a deep purple, dark blue and pastel blue.

PART FOUR:
ASSEMBLING A QUILT

A BASIC BORDER

The edging around a quilt top can be quite plain or worked as intricately as the top pattern itself. It can also be used to harmonize the colours that it frames.

A basic border consists of four strips with no mitring at the corners. Cut to any width, it can be used to increase the overall quilt size without making extra patchwork or quilting work (see p. 98 and the classic frame quilt).

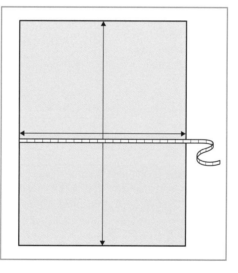

1 Measure across the middle in both directions. Cut four border strips, including a 7mm [¼ in] seam allowance. Cut two to the length of the patchwork; the other two to the same width plus that of two border strips (see step 3).

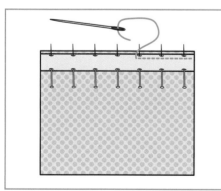

2 Take the lengthways strips first. Pin RS together to the mid-point, then outwards to either end. Tack [baste] firmly before stitching. Press.

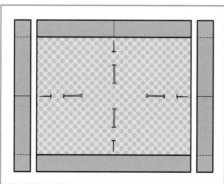

3 Line up the shorter strips, pin, and tack [baste] to the main piece as in Step 2.

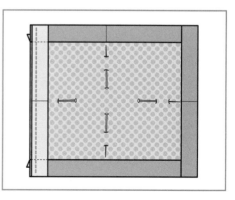

4 Sew the remaining strips straight across the ends of the first two, to form a square joint. Press.

FINISHING

Fold-over edge

This is the simplest finish of all. Trim the top, wadding [batting] and lining level all round. Fold the lining fabric and wadding [batting] back together by 15 mm [⅝ in]. Pin or tack [baste] to hold them in position if necessary. Turn the top edge under once to meet the folded edge of the lining. Slip stitch the top and lining together.

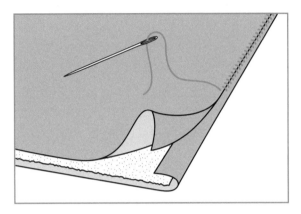

Self-bound edge

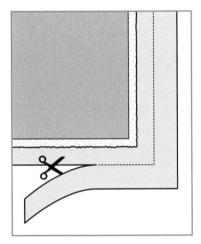

1 With the top and wadding [batting] already trimmed level, cut the lining with an allowance of 2.5–5 cm [1-2 in] all round.

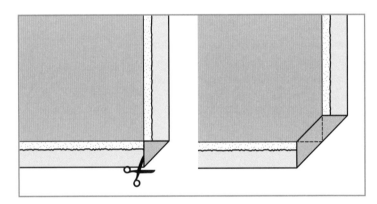

2 Fold, cut, and fold again each corner of the lining, in preparation for mitring.

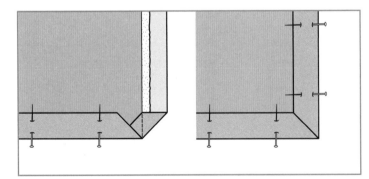

3 Fold the lining upwards to meet the quilt top and form a self-binding. Turn the raw edges under and pin adjacent sides, with the corners meeting in a neat diagonal line.

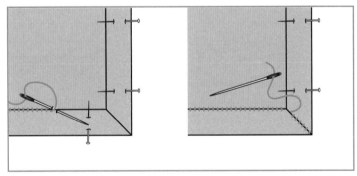

4 Using matching thread, slip stitch the binding to the quilt top all round, closing each mitred corner as you go.

Straight-bound edge

Measure the quilt both ways and add 5 cm [2 in] to the length and width. On the grain (p. 66), cut four binding strips 4–5 cm [1½–2 in] wide. Press a turning of 7 mm [¼ in] down one side of each strip.

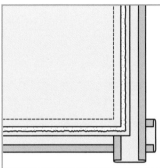

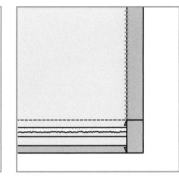

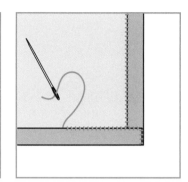

1 RS together, align the unturned edge with the raw edge of the quilt top. Machine stitch together with a 7 mm [¼ in] seam allowance. Prepare all four sides like this.

2 Fold the pressed edge of the binding over to the WS. Pin and slip stitch the first length to the lining fabric, covering the initial stitch line.

3 Fold in the edge of the adjacent binding. Trim away bulk if necessary.

4 Fold the binding up to cover all raw edges. Slip stitch to the lining fabric as in Step 2 and close the squared corner. Repeat around the quilt.

Bias-bound edge

Bias binding is often used on quilted items that cannot be neatened by turning. It can be homemade from steam-pressed bias strips to your chosen width, or bought readymade in various widths and materials.

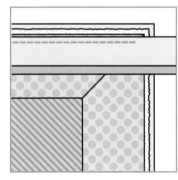

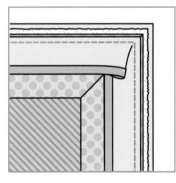

1 Press open one side of the bias binding. RS together, align with the raw edge of the quilt top. Pin and stitch along the fold line of the binding.

2 Carry on sewing right round the quilt. The bias (p. 8) will stretch around the corners. Fold the binding over to the WS. Pin and slip stitch to the lining fabric, covering the initial stitch line.

Signing your quilt

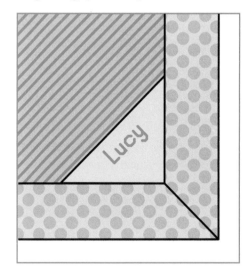

As a finishing touch, embroider your name onto the quilt. Work it into the border, or make a separate label that can be slipstitched to the lining or bound neatly into one corner, as shown here.

PROJECT: A CLASSIC FRAME QUILT

The 'frame' quilt was a clever device of early quiltmakers for creating an eye-catching quilt when they had only a relatively small piece of an interesting printed fabric but a surplus of something more average-looking.

They would take the interesting piece of fabric as the centre of the quilt top and then use strips of complementary fabrics to 'frame' it. Not only was this a pleasing way to feature a favourite fabric, it was also a very quick and simple way to make a quilt.

It is not necessary to use a novelty fabric as the centre piece unless you have one you are keen to use. The project described here features quite an ordinary centre panel but it is nevertheless an eye-catching quilt. You could substitute any fabrics to match a particular colour scheme, if desired.

The finished quilt is approximately 100 cm [40 in] square. If you would like to make it larger, you need to add extra strips to the frame and enlarge the backing and wadding accordingly. It can be sewn by hand or machine but would obviously take much less time using a sewing machine.

Use 100 per cent cotton fabric and thread. The quantities below allow a little extra material for small cutting errors. All strips include a 7 mm [¼ in] seam allowance. The quilt top uses three different-patterned fabrics (A, B and C) and a fourth one (D) of equivalent texture and weight for the quilt backing. All fabrics involved should be pre-shrunk (p. 66).

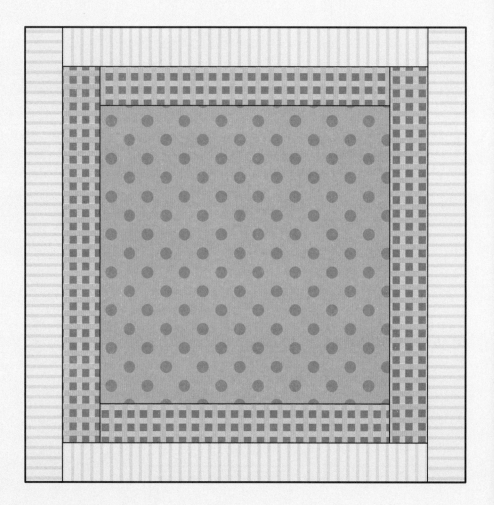

You will need:

- **Fabric A (spot)** One 66 cm [26 in] square, which forms the centre panel
- **Fabric B (check/plaid)** 92 x 56 cm [36 x 22 in]
- **Fabric C (stripe)** 112 x 56 cm [44 x 22 in]
- **Fabric D (backing)** 112 cm [44 in] square
- **Wadding [batting]** 112 cm [44 in] square (final size)
- Cotton thread for machine or hand sewing
- Embroidery thread and needle for tying

Method

Using your cutting mat, acrylic ruler and rotary cutter, from Fabric A cut out the central panel 62.2 cm [24½ in] square.

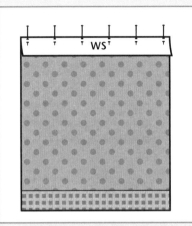

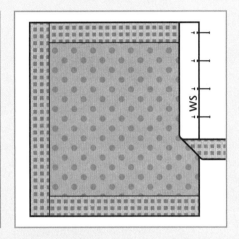

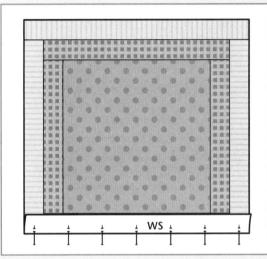

1 Cut two strips of Fabric B, 11.5 x 62.2 cm [4½ x 24½ in]. RS together, pin along two opposite sides of the central panel. Stitch both strips to the panel. Press seams outwards towards the open edges.

2 Measure and cut two more strips of Fabric B, 11.5 x 82.5 cm [4½ x 32½ in]. As before, RS facing, pin then stitch the strips along the remaining two sides of the central panel. Press seams outwards towards the open edges.

3 Take Fabric C, cut two strips 11.5 x 82.5 cm [4½ x 32½ in] and two more 11.5 x 103 cm [4½ x 40½ in]. Attach them in opposite pairs to the preceding frame, as for the central panel. Press seams outwards and then press the entire quilt top.

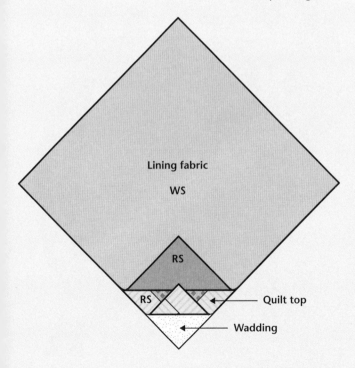

Lining fabric
WS
RS
RS
Quilt top
Wadding

4 Measure and cut a piece 112 cm [44 in] square of the wadding [batting] and also of the backing, Fabric D. Smooth out the wadding [batting] and lay the quilt top RS up on top of it. The top will be slightly smaller all round than the wadding [batting]. Place the piece of backing RS down onto the quilt top.

Pin the three layers all around the perimeter, smoothing them as you go, carefully aligning the edges of the quilt top with the backing. Stitch around the perimeter of the backing fabric with 7 mm [¼ in] seam allowance but leave an opening of about 30 cm [12 in]. Ensure you are sewing right through the quilt back, top and wadding [batting].

Use your rotary cutter, mat and ruler to trim any bits of wadding protruding beyond the quilt top. Snip the four corners and turn it all RS out. Smooth all three layers outwards from the centre. Close the 30 cm [12 in] opening by hand.

Quilting

This quilt lends itself to tufting [tying] (p. 75) at intervals of 15 cm [6 in] along the seam lines and also on the front and central panel, which is the quickest method. Use the acrylic ruler to mark the quilt top at regular intervals. If you would like to quilt more ornately, choose template pattern(s) or filler lines (p. 78) and hand or machine quilt.

THE APPLIQUÉ TRADITION

Examples of appliqué exist from medieval times in Europe
and the technique goes back as far as the Ancient Egyptians.

Although it can be utilitarian, a means to repair holes or tears, appliqué evolved into a decorative art as needleworkers became ever more imaginative, assisted by new products coming onto the market. The 'album' quilt in North America was a special kind. Each block showed a picture on a particular subject, for example a Bible story, a political event or even a mourning quilt, to mark someone's death. More cheerfully, there were friendship album quilts, where friends contributed a block and embroidered their signatures. They often became a family's best quilts because so much time and thought went into making them.

Early appliqué shapes included ordinary domestic objects, simply traced around to provide a template: coins, scissors, eyeglasses or a spoon. Broderie Perse, popular in the eighteenth and nineteenth centuries in the UK and America, consisted of cutting out figures featured on printed fabrics, to appliqué them onto and thus enhance a plain fabric. The name came from the belief that it resembled Persian embroidery.

The Rose of Sharon pattern frequently appeared on American bridal quilts. Complex appliqué like this involves careful planning; the plans show the stitching order for the rose motif and swag border. Repeat shapes are cut from paper or card templates, based on original drafts on graph paper.

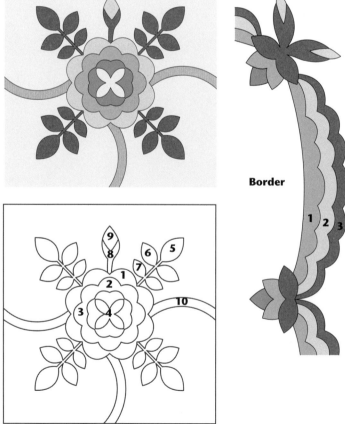

Border

DISPLAY

To display your work as a wall hanging, maybe in an exhibition, you must have some way of suspending it. To construct a hanging sleeve or tube, you can either make it the width of the entire quilt or have a series of smaller ones. Using a fabric that matches or co-ordinates with the backing, cut a strip 26 cm [10 in] deep and as wide as the quilt, plus 10 cm [4 in] extra for hemming.

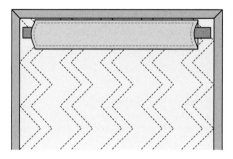

Create a tube by folding fabric RS facing and sewing up the long side. Fold down the raw edges by 5 cm [2 in] at either end and hem stitch. Turn RS out and press so that the seam line will not be noticeable from the back of the quilt. Using a ruler, mark the line on the back of the quilt where you will attach the top of the sleeve, approximately 2.5-5 cm [1-2 in] from the top edge. You cannot machine the sleeve to the quilt, so you must attach it by hand with a suitable stitch such as regular running stitch, back stitch, slip stitch or herringbone. First, sew the top of the sleeve across the width of the quilt then attach the lower side of the sleeve in the same way. Slide the supporting pole through the open ends.

(For stretching and mounting smaller pieces ready for framing, see p. 59).

AFTERCARE

Look for the care symbols on any fabric that you buy; the manufacturer's care label appears on the bolt and you should ask for a care ticket to take away with you. Other points of reference are your own washing machine and tumble dryer manuals.

An extensively hand quilted project is better hand-washed although it can be washed in a machine on a delicate cycle with a spin at low speed and dried outdoors. A quilt can be laundered in the bath, but to reduce the risk of the weight of water breaking threads when lifting out, put the quilt inside a single duvet cover. Squeeze out as much water as you can with hands or feet, then let the duvet cover take the weight as you remove the quilt from the bath. Use clean towels to absorb some of the moisture and allow to dry outdoors on a sheet laid on the grass in warm weather, but place it in the shade as sun may cause certain colours to fade.

Synthetic wadding [batting] is machine washable and can be tumble dried; make certain the quilt top and backing can be treated the same. On the other hand, cotton wadding [batting] should always be pre-shrunk. Some quilters use it straight from the roll deliberately because when they wash the finished quilt, it will dry with an antique puckered effect.

If you have used lightweight woollens or silk in your quilting, and you want to wash it either by hand or machine, choose soap flakes or a liquid for delicates. The cleansing agents in liquid soaps are designed to work at low temperatures and won't leave a powdery deposit. Test strong colours (especially reds) for colourfastness and if in any doubt dry clean the quilt. Woollen or wool-mix fabrics of any kind should always be rinsed in warm water. Use the machine-washable wool setting on your machine, not the low-temperature or hand-wash program that delivers a cold rinse.

Tumble dryers are frequent contributors to accidental shrinkage, some fabrics are better left to dry without heat. Lift your quilt from the washing machine and use a clean towel to remove excess water. Lay the quilt to dry flat or drape it over a drying rack. If necessary, iron fabrics according to the recommended heat setting. Take extra care with trimmings; nylon lace, metallic threads and plastic sequins will shrivel at the touch of a hot iron.

Dust, dirt and perspiration harm fibres of all kinds, and both moths and moulds feed readily on dirt. Put quilts away clean and dry, folded neatly in chests and cupboards, or inside zipped cotton covers for long-term storage. Shake them out occasionally and roll or refold a different way to prevent permanent creases. Avoid the risk of mould or mildew by never storing fabrics in poorly ventilated, damp or humid surroundings such as lofts, basements or neglected cupboards. Low-powered heaters and dehumidifiers help to combat damp and condensation.

GLOSSARY

Appliqué the technique of stitching one fabric on top of another to create designs

Backing the quilt lining

Betweens needles for fine stitching and quilting

Bias any diagonal line between lengthwise and crosswise grains

Bias binding packaged ready-made, in a variety of colours, it is useful for creating appliquéd shapes, especially curves, such as flower stems and basket handles

Block pieced units sewn separately and later assembled into an overall pattern

Bodkin a blunt-tipped, large-eyed needle used for threading cord, ribbon and so on

Border fabric edging or frame added to the top layer of a quilt

Broderie Perse the technique of cutting out a motif from a printed fabric in order to appliqué it onto a plain fabric. The term is French for 'Persian embroidery'.

Calico a plain white cotton cloth, sometimes unbleached, useful for quilt backings

Candlewick a soft, thick cotton embroidery thread

Contour quilting where the parallel lines of quilt stitches are sewn approximately 7mm [¼ in] from the seam lines. Also known as 'outline stitching', emphasizing the geometric shapes in a patchworked block

Cord a cord made from cotton, used in corded quilting. Can be bought by the metre

Echo quilting where the quilting lines echo the shape of each appliquéd shape or patchwork piece. Similar to contour quilting.

Fat quarter half a yard of fabric cut off the bolt then cut in half again along the lengthwise grain to produce a rectangle

Feed-dogs consist of tiny metal teeth that move the fabric from front to back as machine stitching proceeds

Felt non-woven fabric made from compressed fibres. Better quality felt contains wool. Available in many bright colours but bright sunlight will cause some fading in time

Free motion quilting a method of machine quilting with the feed-dogs lowered. It produces filling stitches rapidly

Filling padding sewn between quilt top and backing

Filling stitch a quilting stitch used to cover larger areas of fabric. Can be done by hand or machine

Freezer paper originally a food wrapping, used by quilters to create appliquéd shapes

Fusible web iron-on synthetic bonding material, useful for appliqué

Grain direction in which the warp and weft threads lie

Hawaiian motif a formalized style of appliqué where intricate designs, cut from folded paper, are used as a template to make an appliquéd motif sewn onto a white background and frequently echo-stitched

Hem folded and stitched edge, to prevent fraying

In the ditch quilting stitches made in the centre of the seam

Interfacing extra fabric sewn or ironed between fabric layers to provide more body

Isometric paper paper printed in a grid of equilateral triangles, useful for devising patchwork patterns

Jump stitch a stitch taken to 'jump' across a join or from one part of a design to another, particularly when 'in the ditch' or contour quilting

Kantha a type of embroidery originating in India, consisting primarily of a running stitch. The name comes from 'kontha', meaning 'rags' in ancient Sanskrit

Lawn a fine cotton fabric with a soft feel

Latticing narrow strips used to separate quilt blocks. Also called 'sashing'

Mitre corner pieces joined at an angle of 45 degrees

Motif a distinctive design element

Muslin a sheer, loose-woven cotton fabric. In the US, it is the name given to calico and various sturdy cotton fabrics of plain weave that are good for quilt backings

Nap texture or design that runs in one direction only

Needle (verb) to stitch or stab with a needle

Notch small triangular cut-outs in the seam allowance, for aligning pieces when sewing

Patch a shaped piece of fabric, often cut out with the aid of a template for patchwork

Patchwork fabric shapes or patches sewn together in a set design

Perle [pearl] thread shiny cotton embroidery twist, non-divisible

Piecing joining fabric shapes or patches together

Pile soft raised surface on velvet, corduroy etc (see **Nap**)

Post small square piece at the junction of sashing/lattice strips

Press often used for 'ironing' but more strictly involves steam and a pressing cloth

Presser foot part of the needle assembly that holds fabric flat while the machine needle makes stitches

Quilt bed cover consisting of two layers of fabric with padding sewn or tied between

Quilting action of stitching the three layers of a quilt together

Quilting hoop portable frame for holding a portion of quilt while stitching

RS right side of fabric

Reverse appliqué a technique where several layers of fabric are put together then parts of the upper layer(s) are cut away to reveal those below (*see rear cover*).

Ric rac a type of zig-zag braiding, useful for appliqué

Rose of Sharon a complex appliqué pattern of floral motifs and swags, popular in US bridal quilts

Rotary cutter a very sharp tool with replaceable blades of various diameters, used for cutting fabric strips and trimming wadding

Sashiko traditional Japanese type of embroidery

Sashing narrow strips used to separate quilt blocks. Also called 'latticing'

Scaling proportional enlargement or reduction of a design

Seam allowance distance between the cut edge and the seam line

Seam ripper small sharp tool for removing machine stitching

Selvedge [selvage] solid edge of a woven fabric

Seminole strip-pieced technique often used for borders

Setting in fitting one piece into an angle formed by two others already joined

Sharps general sewing needles

Slip stitch attaches a folded edge to a flat surface

String technique of creating a solid fabric from sewn strips

Strip technique of pattern-building based on strips of fabric rather than blocks

Tacking [basting] temporary stitches made with running stitch, removed when work is finished

Template an outline guide for tracing and cutting

Tension refers to the pressure placed on the needle and bobbin thread by the sewing machine and registered by two types of tension: the thread and bobbin tensions. Read your sewing machine manual for specifics

Tied [tufted] method of securing quilt layers with knots of thread

Top patterned top layer of a patchwork quilt

Trapunto a stuffed quilting technique where motifs are padded so they appear in relief against the background fabric

Vilene see **Interfacing**

WS wrong side of fabric

Wadding [batting] padding in the centre layer of a quilt

Warp runs lengthwise, parallel to the selvedge [selvage]

Weft runs at right angles to the selvedge [selvage]

BEADWEAVING

Since the earliest days of humankind and in all societies, the urge to make art and to decorate one's body has been a constant theme – and drilling holes in shells, bones and pieces of wood so that they could be threaded on a cord was a way of making jewellery that required no technology and few resources. From those primitive beginnings eventually came the vast array of beads and styles of using them that we have today.

Making bead jewellery is endlessly satisfying and can be done by anyone blessed with a little patience and ability to find pleasure in crafting beautiful objects with their hands. In out modern world, where so much depends on digital technology, it is a joy in itself to sit down with some beads, some thread and a few simple tools, and fashion something pretty to adorn someone's neck or wrist.

Weaving beads on a loom gives you the ability to make intricate patterns for belts, bracelets, chokers, handbags, decorations for cushions and many other uses. You may want to invent your own patterns or copy designs that you like, adapting them to fit onto graph paper with each square representing a bead; easiest of all, you can now use computer software to turn any image into a graph pattern.

Whether you plan to work with beads just for pleasure or have an eye to making jewellery to sell, the following pages could provide you with a grounding in how to make a successful start. While the equipment needed isn't complicated, it's always best to get the right tool for the job to avoid frustrating delays and perhaps damage your beads.

Buying the beads, of course, is much more fun. Beading is now a popular craft and there are many well-stocked bead stores to be found – and with the benefit of the internet, you can buy beads worldwide.

Eventually, you may realize you have discovered a new career, or you may simply have developed an addiction to beading for pleasure! Whichever is the case, the journey will be a fascinating one.

PART ONE:
EQUIPMENT AND MATERIALS

Beading is now a popular craft and the variety of beads available is correspondingly wide. While it's possible to buy extensively online, if there's a well-stocked bead shop near you it's best to go in person to make your selections so that you can see the true colours and surface quality of the beads. You'll probably also find that it stimulates ideas for jewellery in a way that scrolling down a web page of catalogued items never will.

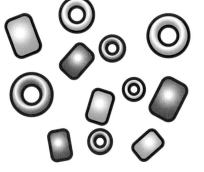

SEED BEADS
These are the small beads used for weaving, though they have many other purposes too, from delicate necklaces and earrings to acting as decorative spacers between larger beads. They vary in size – which is, confusingly, graded differently according to their country of origin – and may be sold in strings, packets or tubes and other plastic containers. You'll find them in a range of qualities and finishes, including opaque, transparent, gloss, matt, lustre, iridescent and metallic, making them suitable for any style of jewellery, from evening wear to folk art.

CUBE BEADS
Another variation in small beads is the cube shape, which provides straight edges in a design rather than the softer, rounded shapes of standard seed beads. You will also find triangular beads on sale, along with other geometric shapes such as hexagons.

CONTAINERS
It's important to take care that your beads are stored in separate containers, since if they become mixed up you will waste a lot of time trying to sort them out again – especially if you're using seed beads. Some are sold in bags, others in containers, and the latter may or may not be suitable for longterm use. It's not difficult to source small plastic containers, ideally with screwtops so that the jar can be held steady while you take the top off; try to find clear ones so that you can see at a glance the colour of the beads inside. Also add a label giving details of colour, size, type and where they are available to save time when you need to buy some more.

POLYESTER AND SILK THREAD
Polyester thread is easily available from craft stores in a range of colours and thicknesses, including a fine one for beadweaving. You will generally need to use a needle for threading, though it's possible to give a rigid end to the thicker threads by waxing them. Silk and embroidery threads have attractive finishes and a greater range of colours, but lack the strength of the synthetic threads.

FINDINGS

The term 'findings' is used for the small items you will need for assembling most of your jewellery.

JUMP RINGS AND SPLIT RINGS
Small and simple, jump rings are probably the findings you will use the most. Just a metal ring with a split in it, a jump ring can be employed to link lengths of threading material or chain together, or to attach fastenings of all kinds. Split rings are similar but coiled like a key ring, making them more secure; this means they can be used as a ring to hook a clasp to.

S-hook clasps are easy to attach, making them useful for necklaces. If you want to make the length of the necklace adjustable you can finish the other end with a length of chain so that the clasp can be hooked into different links. However, as S-hook clasps are not fully closed they are less suitable for bracelets as they may come undone.

Bolt rings are secure but quite fiddly to use, especially as they are usually small. They are not a good choice for someone with arthritic fingers or limited mobility in their arms.

Parrot, trigger, or lobster claw clasps are generally easier to use than bolt rings as they are more solid. They come in a range of metals, finishes and designs.

Magnetic clasps are the easiest of all to attach, but better suited to necklaces than bracelets as they may also attach themselves to metal objects as the wearer goes out and about. Note that magnetic clasps should never be worn by anyone with a pacemaker.

Slider clasps, also known as tube bar clasps, are available in different lengths and with a variable number of loops, making them versatile for multi-strand necklaces and bracelets. One side of the fastening simply slots into the other and locks into place.

Box clasps tend to be traditional in appearance and are available for single or multi-strand pieces. One side of the clasp is a tongue that slides into the decorative side and locks into place, making it a secure fastening.

Barrel, or screw, clasps are very secure but require two hands to tighten them properly, so are unsuitable for bracelets.

Toggles are very easy to use and the range of colours, materials and designs is very large. To attach the clasp the toggle is pulled through the ring, so if you are using large beads you will need to add a few at the end of your necklace or bracelet that are smaller than the ring.

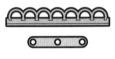

SPACER BARS AND END BARS
For use with multistrand necklaces or bracelets, these may be quite plain or more ornamental. Spacer bars are, as you might expect, a way of keeping the strands spaced apart; end bars have a fastening or just a loop to which a fastening can be attached.

END CONES
These come in a range of designs and are an attractive way to finish multistrand pieces.

CRIMPS
To finish the ends of wire or thread you will need to use crimps, which are slipped on and tightened with pliers.

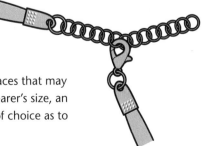

LEATHER CRIMPS AND SPRING ENDS
These are used to finish the ends of leather and fabric cord, with a loop to which you can attach a fastener.

CALOTTES
Calottes are a form of crimp, concealing the end of your thread but with a loop too for the fastening to attach to. They are hinged at the side or the bottom.

SAFETY PINS
An easy way of making informal, contemporary jewellery, safety pins are easily available but can be bought in bead stores in a range of colours for decorative effect.

EXTENSION CHAIN
For making bracelets or necklaces that may need to be adjusted to the wearer's size, an extension chain gives plenty of choice as to the exact length.

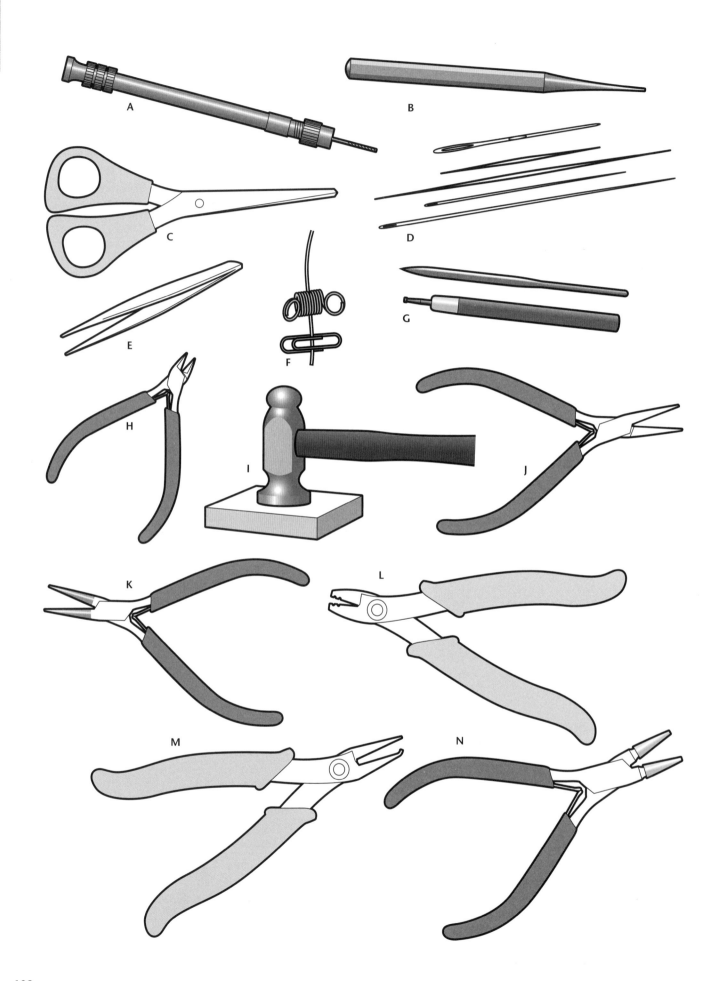

A

B

C

D

E

F

G

H

I

J

K

L

M

N

TOOLS

Some of the tools needed for making bead jewellery can be found in DIY stores, while for others you will need to visit bead stores, either in person or online. It's worth getting exactly the right equipment, as a few pounds saved in purchases can add up to hours of unnecessary fiddling and perhaps damaged beads or fastenings too.

A Reamer
This is an important piece of equipment, especially if you will be using seed beads for weaving. This handy tool comes with a variety of diamond-tipped files for smoothing and enlarging the holes in your beads where necessary. Always keep the files and beads wet while using, partly to prevent damage to the bead and reamer but also to avoid breathing in harmful dust.

B Awl
You will need to move knots along your threads to get them placed exactly right, and using an awl is the best way to do it. Another implement such as a large needle or cocktail stick can be used as a substitute, but the large handle of the awl makes the job easier.

C Scissors
Ordinary household scissors will suffice, as long as they are sharp. For close work, a small pair with sharply pointed blades will be easiest to manoeuvre.

D Needles
For some tasks, such as stringing large beads, strong, blunt-ended needles that can be bought in a haberdashery department will suffice, but for beadweaving you will need to buy long, extra-fine needles from a bead store. There you will also find needles that have a long eye running down the centre, which are much easier to thread.

E Tweezers
Fine-pointed tweezers are invaluable for unpicking knots and picking up small beads. The ones sold in bead stores are best suited for the job.

F Bead stopper
You will want to make sure that when you are working with beads they are not going to fall off the end of your thread. A bead stopper is a handy little device, although in the absence of one a paper clip will do.

G Files
The end of a length of metal wire will need to be smoothed to avoid it scratching the wearer. An emery board will suffice, but as always the proper tool will save time and a metal file from a bead shop is preferable. A wire rounder, which has a cup burr at the tip, is ideal for rounding the end of a wire; just insert the wire into the cup and turn the wire rounder back and forth. Don't use it for memory wire, though, as this will destroy the inside of the cup.

H Wire cutters
So that you can get in close to your work, buy wire cutters with small, pointed ends. Memory wire is so strong it will ruin ordinary wire cutters; use cutters intended for the purpose, or heavy-duty cutters from a DIY store.

I Hammer and block
Hammering wire gives it interesting texture and shape. The best hammer to buy is one that is flat at one end and rounded at the other, and you will also need a steel block to lay the wire on.

J Flat-nose pliers
These pliers have flat jaws and are used for myriad purposes, such as attaching findings and fastenings and making angles in wire.

K Round-nose pliers
As the name suggests, round-nose pliers have rounded jaws that taper to a point. Use them for making wire loops; if you wish to make a series of loops of the same size, mark the jaws to help you wrap the wire round in the same place each time.

L Crimping pliers
These have two notches in the jaws, one to squeeze your crimp and the other to fold it neatly over. While flat-nose pliers can be used for crimping, it's easy to flatten the crimp too much.

M Split-ring pliers
Split rings are very fiddly to open, so if you are going to use them a lot it's worth investing in pliers with a tip designed to open them.

N Nylon jaw pliers
The softer surface of these pliers makes them suitable for straightening wire and working with aluminium wire, which is soft and easily damaged.

PART TWO

BEADWEAVING METHODS AND TECHNIQUES

THE BEAD LOOM

Looms are available in wood, plastic or metal and in a range of sizes and designs. If you are handy at DIY, or have an obliging partner or friend who is, a bead loom is very simple to make; just a frame with nails or the upright teeth of a metal comb round which to warp threads at each end will allow you to get started. A winding mechanism is more tricky to make, but if your frame is quite long you can create a lot of pieces without needing to wind the work round rollers. However, if you find you really enjoy beadweaving, a handsome and sturdy wooden loom will add to your pleasure.

SETTING UP A LOOM
The first step in beadweaving is to set up the warp threads on your loom. There are two methods of doing this: individual warp or single warp, also known as pulled warp or endless warp. The latter method avoids the task of finishing off a number of threads, but you'll need to take great care when working that you don't put your needle through a warp thread; to finish the work you need to pull all the threads through to leave one long thread remaining, and once you have mistakenly anchored a warp thread with a weft thread this becomes impossible to do.

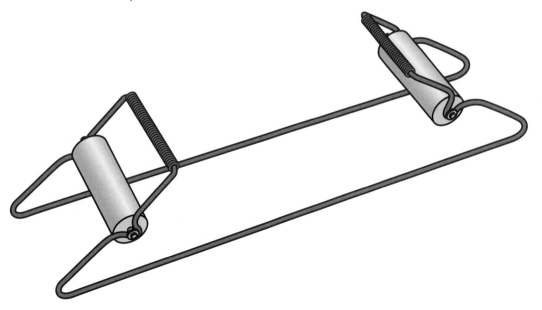

Always consider whether you need to have an odd number of beads in each row – this allows you to have a central bead in your design and also make a buttonhole (p. 121).

Individual warp

Using strong synthetic thread, first cut the warp threads to the length of your proposed piece plus at least 15 cm [6 in] at each end to attach to the loom. You'll need one more thread than the number of beads in a row, and it's a good idea to put two threads at each side – you'll have extra threads to finish off, but the beadwork will be stronger. So, if your design is seven beads across, you'll need ten threads.

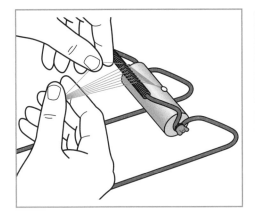
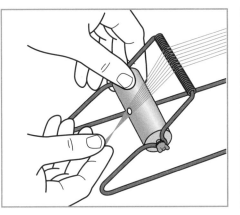
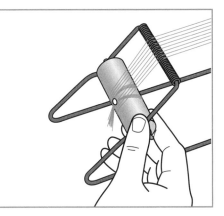

1 Knot the threads together at one end, using an overhand knot. Loop them over the peg provided on your loom and draw them over the grooves or coil above it. Holding them taut, separate them enough to allow the beads you'll be using to fit between them, using an awl, strong needle or other implement that allows you to pick up the threads one by one.

2 Pass the threads over the grooves or coil at the other end of the loom and separate them in the same manner. Tie an overhand knot and hook the threads over the peg (you may find it helpful to put a piece of low tack sticky tape over the threads in the groove or coil to keep them in position while you do this).

3 Adjust the rollers so that there are roughly equal lengths of thread at each end, then tighten one roller. Turn the other until the threads are tautly held, then tighten it.

Single warp

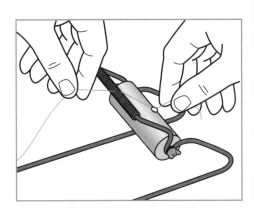
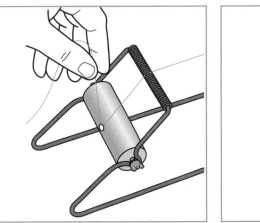
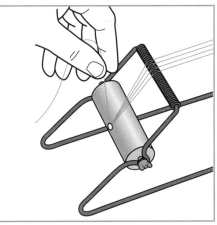

1 You'll need a considerable length of thread for this method, using it straight off the reel. Tie the thread to the peg at one end of the loom, run it through a groove and then take it down to the matching groove at the other end of the loom.

2 Loop the thread round the second peg and then, keeping it taut, take it back down to the end where you started, placing it in the grooves at the correct distance to take your beads. Continue until you have completed a warp of the width your design requires, then tie the thread to the last peg.

STARTING TO WEAVE

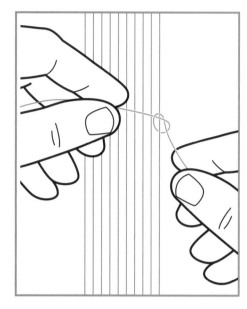

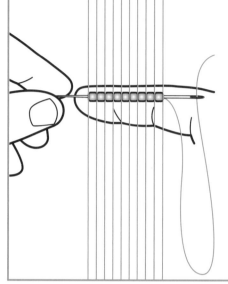

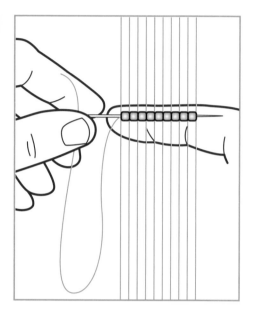

1 First, check that you will be able to pass the needle and thread you plan to use several times – your weft thread can be less sturdy than the warp thread. Thread a length onto a long, fine beading needle, using as much as you feel you can comfortably manage without tangling, so that you don't need to add new thread too often. Using an overhand knot, tie the thread onto the outside warp thread.

2 Following your pattern, pick up the first row of beads on your needle and push them up *under* the warp threads, one bead between each thread. Pull the needle and thread all the way through the beads, keeping your other index finger beneath them for support.

3 Bring needle and weft thread over the outer waro thread. Now pass the needle in the opposite direction, through the beads *above* the warp thread, and pull the thread through until it connects with the warp thread, forming a firm edge.

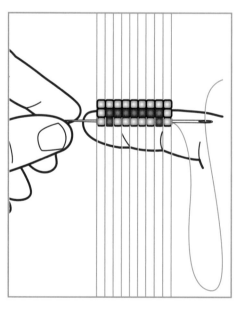

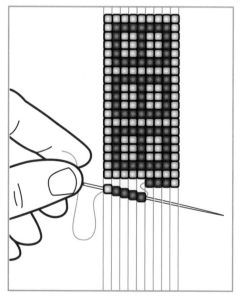

4 Repeat for the following rows, pushing each row of beads snugly up against the previous one as you go.

5 If you run out of thread, knot in a new length between two beads within the row, as the join is less obtrusive than at the edges. Sew in the tails once you have taken the beading off the loom.

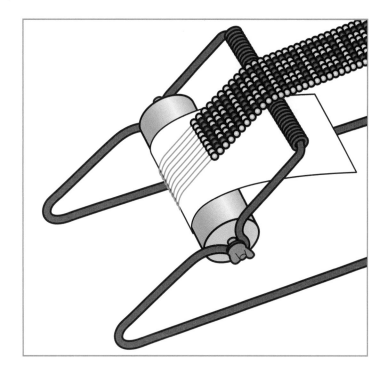

6 If the piece you are making is to be longer than the distance between the grooves that space the warp, loosen the rollers and wind the piece along as far as is necessary. If this means that the beadwork will lie over the peg, provide a little padding in the form of a piece of card.

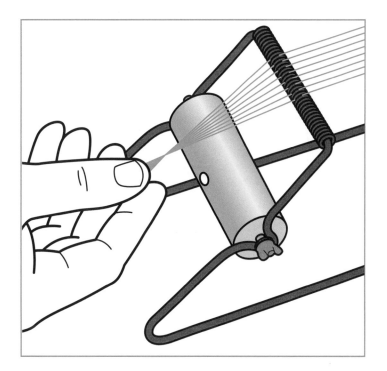

7 To take your work off the loom, simply loosen the rollers and lift the threads clear of the pegs.

INCREASING AND DECREASING

Increasing

Providing variation in the width of your woven piece can be done by simply adding or subtracting the number of beads in a row. If you will be increasing, don't forget to allow for that when you set up your warp threads.

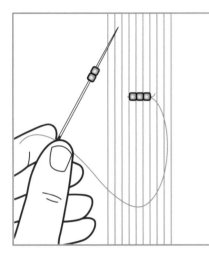 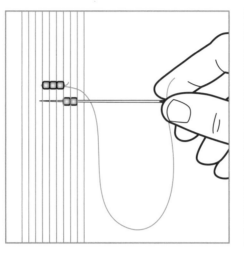 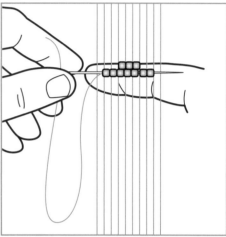

1 At the end of a row, bring the weft thread out above the beads and pick up the number of extra beads you want to increase by.

2 Lay them on top of the warp as an extension to the new row to come, push them down and pass the needle through them beneath the warp threads.

3 Pick up the remaining beads, including any to form a matching increase at the other edge, push them up through the warp and pass the needle back through above the warp, including the beads you first added.

Decreasing

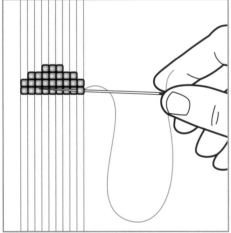 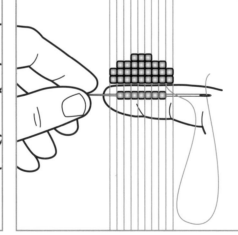 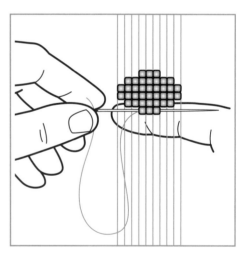

1 After completing the last full-width row, take the needle over the outer warp thread and put it back through the number of beads on that row by which you want to decrease. Bring the needle out at the top then pass it over the new outer thread of the warp to the underside.

2 Pick up the smaller number of beads for the shorter row and weave into place in the usual way.

3 Continue to decrease until the woven beads have reached the shape you want to make.

MAKING AN INTEGRATED FRINGE

While you can add a fringe after your woven panel is finished, it is often easier to do it as you go. If you plan it out on your graph paper along with the rest of the design, you will know exactly the point at which to start adding the fringe.

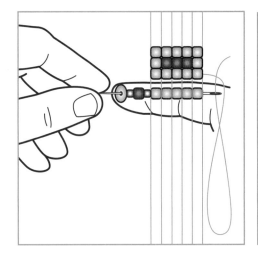

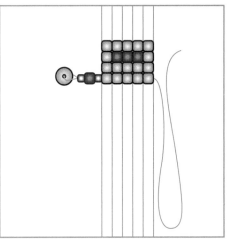

1 When you reach the row of beads where the fringe starts, pick up the additional beads, remembering you will need at least one to pass the thread back round.

2 Supporting the extra beads with your finger, pass the needle round the end bead and then back along the other beads in the fringe and the row on the warp threads.

3 A choker looks good with a graduated shape; just plan your design so that the fringing lengthens and then shortens again once you are past the central point of the choker.

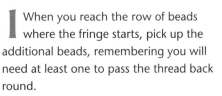

MAKING LOOPED EDGINGS

Loops cannot be integrated and must be added afterwards. However, for stability, you need to thread through the beads on the warp as before.

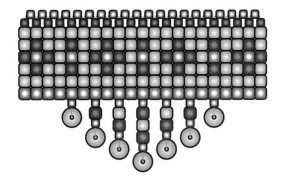

1 Knot in a thread at the top of the row beneath which you want the loop to hang. Pass the needle through the beads on the warp, then pick up the beads for the loop. Thread the needle back up the row where you want the loop to terminate.

2 Continue to add further loops to the design you have chosen; graduated lengths and overlapping loops work well.

FINISHING OFF

When using the individual warp method, you will have numerous tails of thread to deal with to make a neat finish. There are several ways to do this, either disguising them or making a feature of them.

Sewing in

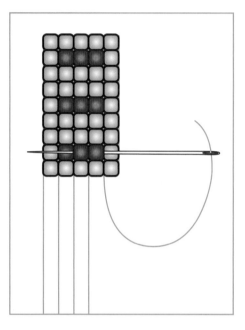

Thread each tail onto a beading needle and pass it through a few beads. Make a knot by taking the needle behind a warp thread in the weaving to make a loop. Pass the needle through the loop and tighten, then thread the needle through a few more beads before trimming off the thread as close to the beadwork as you can. Any tails on the side edges, where you have joined in new thread, can be treated in the same way.

Weaving in

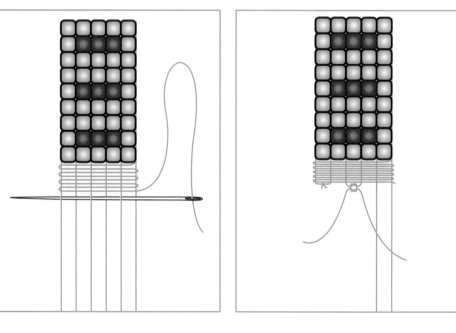

1 Before removing the beadwork from the loom, weave the weft thread in and out of the warp threads to make a panel about 8 mm [¼ in] wide.

2 Lift the beadwork off the loom then tie the warp threads together in pairs. Trim them close to the knots. You can then attach a fastener to the neatly woven panel or, if you are using a backing for your beadwork, fold it beneath the beadwork and cover it with the backing.

Plaiting

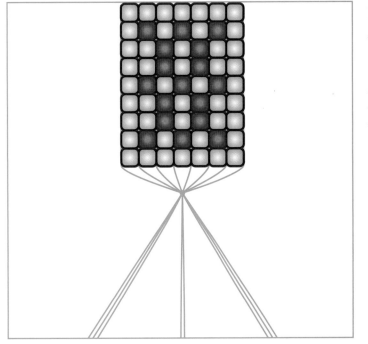

Separate your warp threads into three bundles and plait them neatly, finishing with a knot. It doesn't matter if the number of threads isn't exactly divisible by three as they aren't thick enough for the disparity to be evident.

Weaving to the centre

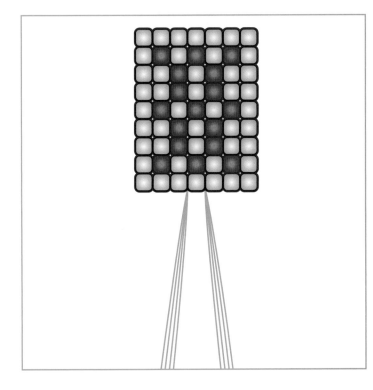

Weave your warp threads through the beads at the end of the piece so that they all exit from the centre. Knot them together and enclose them in a calotte, to which you can then attach a fastener.

FASTENINGS

While the commercial fastenings used for all types of necklaces, chokers and bracelets can be attached to woven bead panels, making a fastening that incorporates beads is a particularly attractive touch.

Loop and toggle

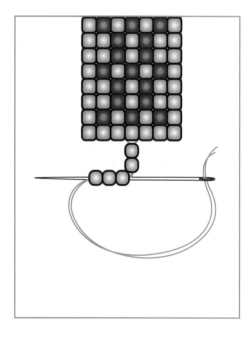

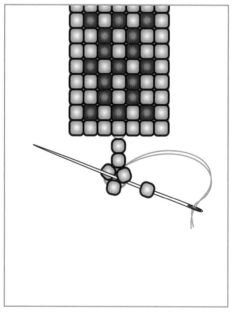

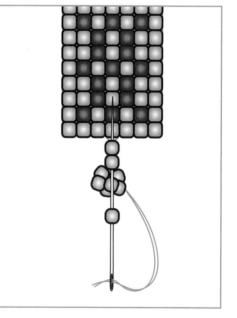

1 When you sew in the warp threads after finishing your weaving (p. 116), leave two threads in the centre of your woven panel. Thread these onto a beading needle, and slip five seed beads on to the thread. Pass the needle back through the last three beads and pull them into a circle.

2 Pick up a single bead with your needle and pass the needle through the circle. Build up a toggle by adding more beads, one at a time, in the same way.

3 To finish, take the threads back through the first two beads that form a stem to the toggle, pass them through a few beads in the woven panel, then knot and trim them.

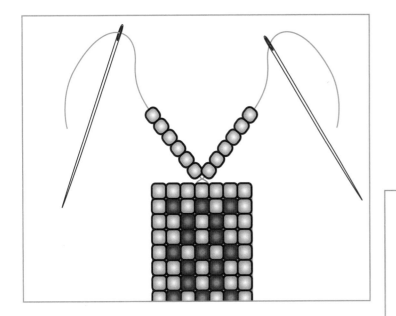

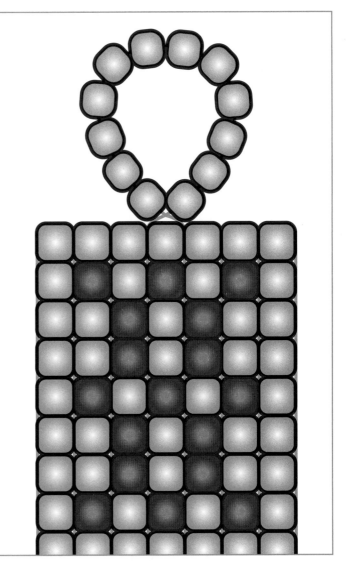

4 At the other end, sew in the warp threads leaving two in the centre as before. Thread them on to two needles and pick up half the beads intended for the loop with each needle – you need a loop big enough to go over the toggle without much difficulty, but not so large that the toggle will slip out.

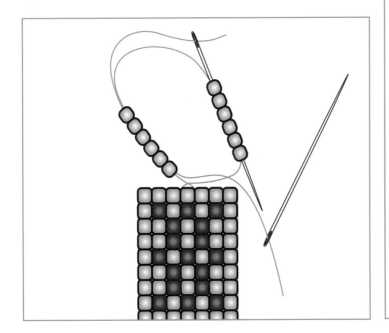

5 Pass each needle through the beads on the opposite thread so that they are all on a double thread; if you wish, pass one needle back through the whole loop to make a stronger three-thread loop. Finish off the tails as in Step 3.

Loop and button

As a variation on a loop and toggle fastening, use a pretty button instead, attached to the woven panel by a short length of single beads; thread a central warp thread on to the needle then pass it through the beads, through the hole in the button and then back down through the beads again.

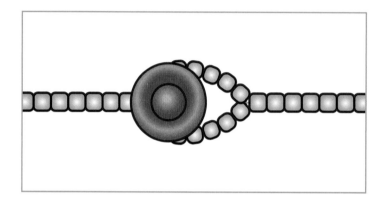

Loop and decorated bead

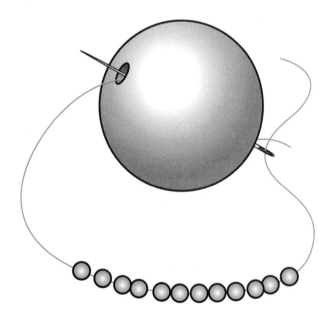

1 Anchor the tail of a long thread then pass it through the hole in a large bead. Pick up enough seed beads to fill the thread as far as the other end of the hole, then pass the needle back round and pick up more beads.

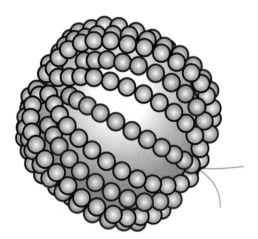

2 Continue until the big bead is largely covered with seed beads, then tie the ends of the thread together. If you wish to have a really solid effect, you can also pick up beads in small numbers at a time and take them round the circumference of the bead, passing the needle through the first set of beads as you go. Make a loop at the other end of the woven panel as before.

Bead and buttonhole

To make a buttonhole in your woven panel, you will need to have an odd number of beads. The slot can only be narrow, so check carefully that you are making it long enough for your bead to pass through it.

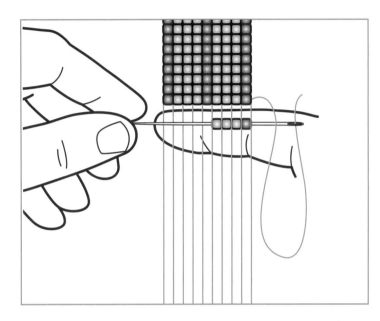

1 Pick up half the normal number of beads (minus the central bead) needed for the row and push them up through the warp threads. Pass the needle through above the warp, then take the needle back again below the warp.

2 Continue to add short rows until you have the necessary length. Weave the thread back through the rows, pulling the needle out at the end of the last full row.

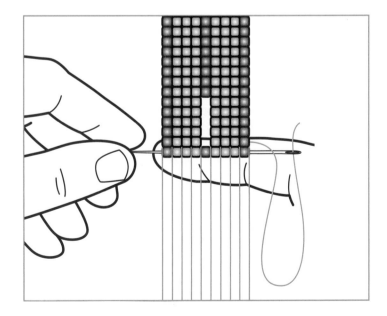

3 Once you have made a matching number of short rows on the other side, bead across the whole width for about three rows to finish making the buttonhole and the woven panel itself.

BEADWEAVING DESIGNS

Mapping out your designs on paper allows you to create a finished diagram to follow when you are weaving beads. Seed bead artists can use ordinary graph paper or try the loom work graph paper available online.

The designs on this page are examples of two very different visual styles, the first sinuous and floral and the second geometric, in the style of Native American and African beadwork, For the first, you could use any type of seed bead, from opaque and bright to translucent and in more subtle colours for a more Victorian feel; for the second, brightly coloured opaque beads are best, partly to stay faithful to the origins of this style and also because they better show the strong geometry of the patterning.

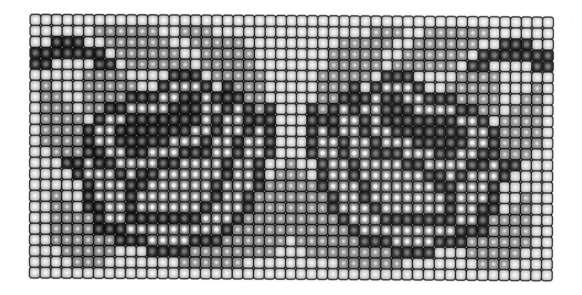

These designs are easy to follow, should you wish to make them; otherwise, just study them as an example of how to work out a pattern of colour and shape on graph paper for your own designs.

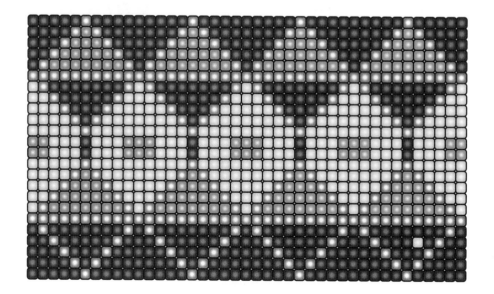

Many needlework patterns are adaptable for use on the beading loom so long as they are laid out on a square grid. This means knitting, crochet, cross stitch and needlepoint could provide you with hundreds of readymade patterns.

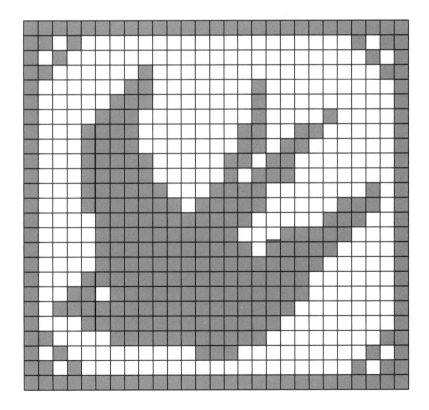

CROSS STITCH

Cross stitch is one of the oldest forms of hand embroidery, popular all over the world and it is little wonder that it remains so. Not only is it easy to learn – cross stitch is usually the first embroidery stitch taught to children – but it's quickly arranged into patterns, pictures and letters by following grid charts where each square represents a single stitch. The pleasure in achievement can become quite addictive as the design grows and different colours are added.

The essentials of counted cross stitch are set out here with plenty of illustrations for guidance. There are sections on equipment and various threads and fabrics, as well as advice on stitching, how to read charts, and sample motifs and alphabets for you to use. The terminology used throughout is UK-standard, but we have included relevant US terms in square brackets [ ] to make this a practical guide for all readers.

The art of cross stitch dates back at least as far as the 6th or 7th century CE when it was used to decorate household linens with floral or geometric patterns, worked simply in black or red thread. Folk costumes, especially from northern and eastern Europe, are often decorated with similar traditional designs. Medieval Assisi work and Tudor blackwork were beautiful, intricate developments of the same technique. Later came the familiar multicoloured sampler, which served several purposes: to record patterns or motifs in the absence of pattern books; to teach children how to stitch; and finally to demonstrate a young woman's prowess with the needle.

Nowadays, we happily incorporate cross stitch designs into many things, from greetings cards to buttons, bookmarks, pot covers and paperweights; while larger projects – including elaborate pre-printed kits – are stitched with skill and patience, to be framed hopefully as future family heirlooms.

PART ONE:
EQUIPMENT AND MATERIALS

NEEDLES AND FABRICS

Needles are manufactured in various thicknesses for different uses. The following chart is a general guide to the size of needle suitable for cross stitch on aida or evenweave fabrics. The higher the number, the finer the needle. Dimensions may vary slightly between manufacturers.

NEEDLE SIZE	FABRIC	NEEDLE LENGTH	EYE LENGTH
18	6 count aida / 10 count evenweave	48 mm	10.0 mm
20	8 count aida	44 mm	9.0 mm
22	11 count aida / 22-25-27 count evenweave	40 mm	8.0 mm
24	14 count aida / 28 count evenweave	36 mm	7.5 mm
26	16 count aida / 32 count evenweave	33 mm	6.5 mm
28	18 count aida / 36-55 count evenweave	28 mm	5.5 mm

Cross stitch is most frequently worked with blunt-tipped tapestry needles, designed to glide through the holes in the fabric weave without splitting the threads. They have long oval eyes to take multiple strands of embroidery cotton [floss] as well as the thicker type of craft threads such as perle [pearl] cotton and tapestry wool.

EQUIPMENT

A Needles

B Fabric

C Thread (including tacking thread)

D Dressmaking shears

E Small sharp scissors

F Thimble

G Laying tool: a small pointed stick
of metal or wood for smoothing and
straightening threads as you stitch (a
large blunt yarn needle will do)

H Masking tape

I Embroidery marker pencil

J Embroidery transfer pencil

K Carbon paper

L Graph paper

M Lamp with daylight bulb

N Magnifying glass

Although not essential, working with
hoops and frames (see p. 15) keeps
the fabric taut and smooth and makes
it easier to see how your work is
progressing.

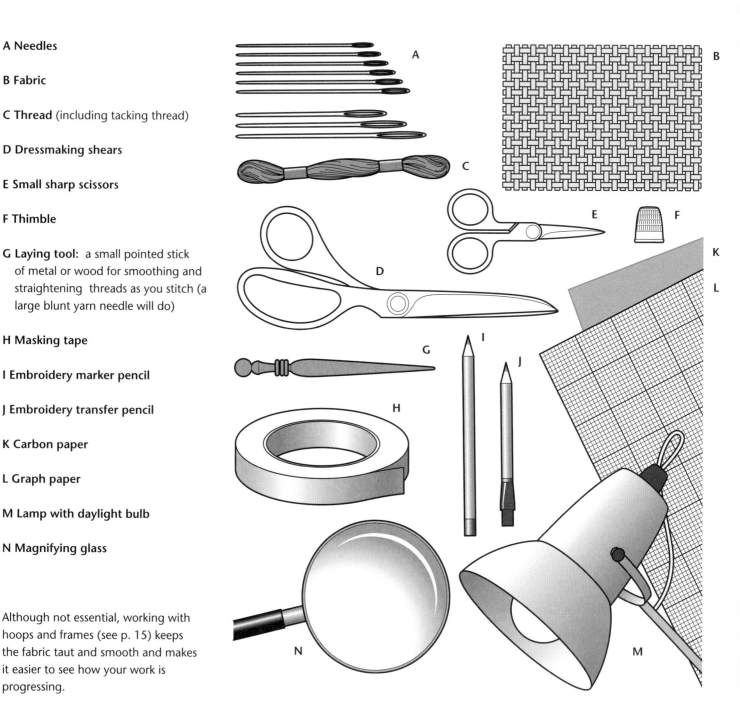

FABRICS AND THREAD COUNTS

The background texture and colour provided by your fabric is important.
The most widely used fabrics for cross stitch are evenweave and aida,
and both come in ranges of neutral tones and colours.

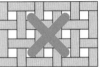

Aida

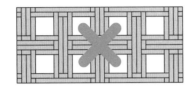

A block weave fabric favoured by beginners because of its regular construction and visible stitch holes. It also has a stiffer finish for hand-held work. Note that unstitched areas have a very distinct texture compared with evenweave, so be sure this is the effect you want.

If the pattern contains fractional stitches (p. 132), you will have to make an additional hole between existing ones by stitching into the solid part of the block weave.

5-, 6- or 8-count A low-count aida for use by children, sometimes called Binca canvas.

11-count Many find that they can work on this when the more usual 14-count becomes too hard on the eyes.

14-count Easy to work and used in more commercial designs than any other fabric.

16-count Gives scope for greater detail than 14-count.

18-count An aida for detailed work. Stitch a small sample before launching upon a large project as you may find this count too demanding for comfort.

22 -count Another aida for really fine work. Traditionally used for Hardanger and also ideal for small projects such as pot lids, paperweights and coasters.

Evenweave

An evenweave is any natural or man-made fabric having the same number of threads per inch (2.5 cm) counted vertically and horizontally; this keeps the cross stitches square and even. It is frequently made either of linen, such as Belfast 32-count and Cashel 28-count or – less expensively – of cotton, such as Linda 27-count and Hardanger 22-count.

Evenweave threads are usually of uniform thickness, although the pure linens are more random. Cross stitch is worked over two threads, so you will be stitching into alternate holes.

The greater the thread count per inch – sometimes given as HPI (holes per inch) – the finer the cloth and the smaller your stitches will be. A 22-count evenweave will yield 11 cross stitches per inch, and a 32-count produces 16.

Evenweave and aida are interchangeable with the aid of a little arithmetic. So if a pattern calls for 28-count evenweave stitched over 2 threads of the fabric, use a 14-count aida and stitch into every hole instead. In the same way, you would replace 32-count evenweave with 16-count aida, and 22-count with 11-count.

Both fabrics are woven in a variety of widths and also in narrow bands with pre-stitched edges, ideal for bookmarks, cakebands, tie-backs and so on.

When calculating the amount of fabric you need for a project, add a clear margin of 10–12 cm (4–5 in) around the outer edges of the design. Allow proportionally less if the design itself is no bigger than a 10–12 cm (4–5 in) square.

CANVAS

You can cross stitch with tapestry wool or stranded cotton [floss] on a cotton or linen canvas. There are four mesh sizes, 10-, 12-, 14- and 18-count, which are compatible with any stitch chart (count the holes in canvas work, not the threads). With a starched finish that gives a firm base to work on, canvas comes as both single thread mesh (mono) and double (duo).

The latter is also called Penelope canvas, which can be used to double your count and – like evenweave – simplifies fractional stitches. Ease the double threads apart first with a thick tapestry needle, then treat each as a single.

Mono canvas

Duo (Penelope) canvas

Plastic canvas

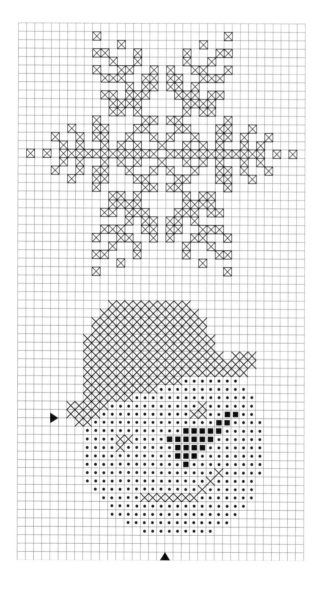

PLASTIC CANVAS

Cut plastic canvas to shape for anything from Christmas tree decorations to coasters, photo frames or boxes. It is available in three forms – standard, rigid and soft – and in various colours as well as 'clear'. Depending on the mesh size (5, 7, 10 or 14 HPI) it may be stitched with stranded embroidery cotton [floss], perle [pearl] thread or double knitting wool [worsted].

Draft the shapes below onto standard canvas with a water-soluble marker. The Snowman can be a coaster or a tree decoration. Cut the canvas and snip off the nubs, any mistakes can be mended with superglue. Wash off the ink. For a shimmering effect, use lurex yarn or combine blending filament with the main thread.

READING AND CREATING CROSS STITCH CHARTS

Cross stitch patterns used to consist only of plain black squares or dots. Now there is a variety of squared charts, including those very usefully printed in full colour.

Here is a simple heart-shaped motif. Each square on the chart represents two threads of evenweave fabric or one block of aida, and each stitch occupies one square.

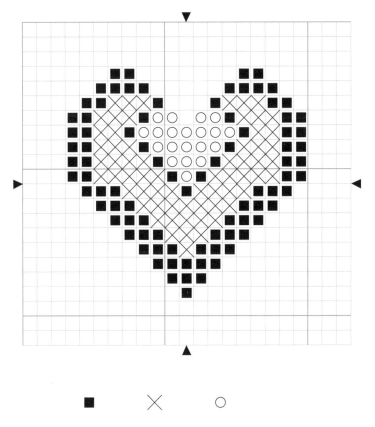

■   ✕   ○

= yellow   x = blue   v = green   o = red

DESIGN SIZE: 23W BY 21H
STICTHING LEVEL: BEGINNER

Mark the centre of each edge of the chart with a small arrowhead. It can be hard to keep your place on a large chart, try dividing it into a grid of manageable sections, marked with a coloured pen.

With larger projects, start stitching in the centre of a design and work outwards. This will ensure even margins at the edges.

Charting your own design

Being able to chart your own design broadens your cross-stitching horizons. Graph paper is required for drafting patterns by hand and you can download grids in various count sizes from online needlecraft sites.

The numbers of stitches from top to bottom and side to side establish the design size; don't forget to include any stitched background area in your calculations. Start by outlining the required number of squares on your chart. For a 30 cm (12 in) design, you will work to 168 (12x14) stitches on 14-count aida. There will be fewer stitches on 11-count: 132 (12x11) and many more stitches on 18-count: 216 (12x18).

Remember that evenweave is worked over two threads and divide the evenweave thread count by two before you begin to calculate the number of stitches required.

You can either colour in your chart or, if you are charting in black and white, decide on a range of symbols as a key.

Small symbols in one corner of a square stand for either a quarter-stitch or three-quarter stitch (p 132).

Digital chartmaking

For some time stitchers have used the graphics program Adobe Photoshop to convert artwork and photographs to digital cross-stitch patterns. Now there's an increasing number of cross- stitch apps available on Androids (smartphones and tablets), including some for free. They often combine related features like patterns, fabric calculators, stitch directories and colour charts from leading thread manufacturers.

PART TWO:
CROSS STITCH METHODS AND TECHNIQUES

PREPARING THREADS

How many strands to use

As a rule, the number of strands of cotton [floss] that you sew with should match the thickness of one thread pulled from the edge of the fabric. Use three or four strands on an 11-count fabric, two or three for a 14-count, and two for an 18-count.

Single strand outline

Many pictorial cross stitch designs are outlined in backstitch, often sewn in black with just one or two strands of cotton [floss].

Separating and recombining stranded cotton [floss]

Multiple strands of cotton [floss] used straight from the skein can produce bumpy stitches so it is worth taking the trouble to separate the strands, smooth them straight and put them together again in the same direction. This will reduce twisting and tangling, and the stitches will lie better.

Grip one strand firmly at the top and draw your other hand down taking the remaining threads with you until the single strand is free. The others will bunch up but won't become knotted. Finally, lay all the strands out straight and reassemble as you wish.

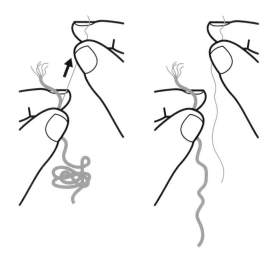

RECORD CARD

At the start of a project, punch a line of holes in a piece of card and loop a 7 cm [3 in] strand from each skein through a separate hole. Write the name of the project in the centre of the card and then label each hole with the appropriate manufacturer's name, shade number and chart symbol. This provides you with a quick reference while you work and a handy hard-copy record once you have finished.

931
327
3721
316
352
501
729
3346

Thread organizer

As well as creating a record card, well-organized stitchers might like to make a similar one for use throughout the project. Cut a thread of each colour to a working length (about 45 cm [18 in]) and loop it through the punched card, where it remains ready for the needle.

Metallic threads tend to twist or break more easily, so it is advisable to cut those into shorter lengths (about 30 cm [12 in]). They also tend to unravel at the ends, which can be stopped with anti-fray fluid. Ends can be prepared in advance on the thread organizer and eventually trimmed off.

PREPARING FABRIC

When you cut a new piece of fabric, remove any selvedges [selvages] and check carefully for faults in the weave before ironing under a clean, dry cloth.

Prepare the raw edges

Linen frays very easily, so does evenweave, aida less so. But whatever the fabric, prepare the raw edges to keep them neat and prevent threads getting caught while you embroider. Here are some options; with 3 and 4, you will have to cut away 1 cm [0.5 in] all round afterwards. Chemicals and adhesives will damage the fabric in the long run.

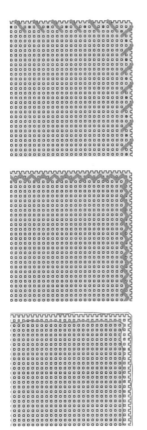

1 Overstitch the edges by hand with sewing cotton. Roll a small hem if you wish.

2 Zigzag stitch round the edges with a sewing machine.

3 Apply fray stopper sparingly and allow to dry.

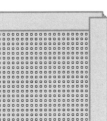

4 Frame with masking tape

With 3 and 4, be aware that you will have to cut away 1 cm [½ in] all round afterwards. Chemicals and adhesives will damage the fabric in the long run.

Tacking guidelines

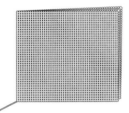

1 Fold the fabric in half twice to find the centre point, crease gently with your fingers and mark with a pin.

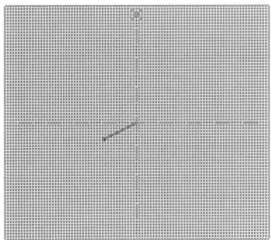

2 Open out and tack [baste] along the folds in a contrasting thread.

Choose a place outside your stitching area and sew a large X to indicate the right side of the work and mark the top.

BASIC STITCHING METHODS

Cross stitch

The most important rule about cross stitch is that all the top stitches go in one direction. It doesn't matter which way as long as they are uniform. Working with separated and recombined strands (p. 130), and smoothing your stitches with a laying tool (p. 126) will help.

There are two cross-stitching methods.

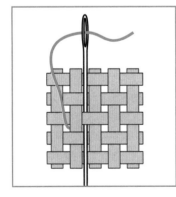

1 The traditional English method completes each X before moving on to the next.

2 The Danish method does the first legs of the Xs first, and completes them as they return along the row.

There are also two ways of stitching. One is the 'stabbing' or 'push and pull' method. There is no alternative when working with a hoop or frame because the fabric is too taut. But if hand-holding, you can manipulate the fabric to use the 'sewing' method below.

Fractional stitches

These are quarter-, half- and three-quarter cross stitches, mainly used to smooth outlines and round corners; although they can give a lighter look to an otherwise solid area, or share a square with another colour.

The half-stitch is the same as the first leg of the Danish method shown left.

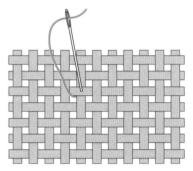

The quarter-stitch is done across one thread only if you are working on evenweave fabric, on aida it must be done as shown below.

Coming up from the lower left corner, cross diagonally and insert the needle into the solid centre of the aida square. Pull the thread right through to the back.

Coming up from the lower right corner, cross diagonally and insert the needle into the hole top left. Pull the thread right through to the back. Coming up from the lower right corner, cross diagonally and insert the needle into the hole top left. Pull the thread right through to the back.

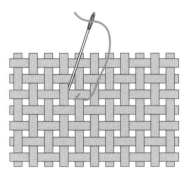

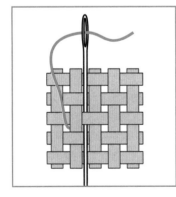
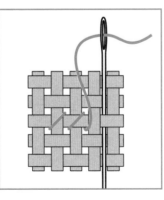
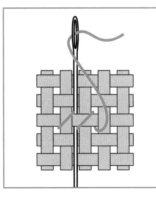
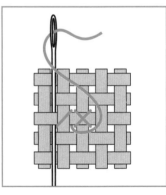

1 On the first leg, in one action, push the needle into the fabric at the top and out of the hole below.

2 Repeat for the remainder of the row.

3 Cross the last stitch diagonally, pushing the needle in at the top and out of the hole directly below.

4 Repeat to the other end of the row where all the crosses will be complete.

Staggered cross stitch

With staggered cross stitch it is possible to achieve a subtle, simpler pattern and save yourself a few stitches. It's particularly useful when stitching very close, narrow diagonals. Begin by working the first row normally. The second row starts offset by an uneven number of threads to one side, so that the needle does not pass through the holes of the row above but those lying in between. The third row starts with an uneven number of threads in relation to the second row, but you will note that the stitches of this row align with those in the first – and so on.

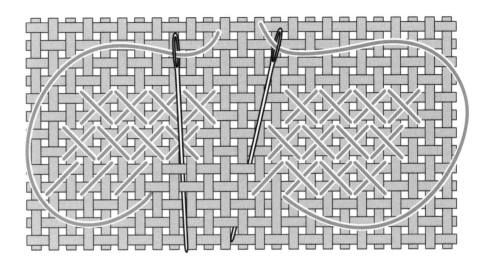

Backstitch

The backstitch has close links with cross-stitch. It is used to define cross-stitched areas and should be done last in order to maintain an unbroken line. Some stitchers prefer to use a finer needle at this stage, it is a thin line and the number of strands is seldom greater than one or two. The thread does not always have to be black, in fact you may achieve a more subtle and pleasing effect with a darker shade of the cross-stitch filler. Start and finish by running the thread under a few cross stitches at the back of your project.

Holbein or double running stitch

A staple stitch of blackwork, this looks like backstitch but is actually constructed from two passes of running stitch, where the second pass returns and precisely fills the gaps left by the first. This makes the back far neater than that of backstitch and ideal on its own for double-sided items such as bookmarks and Christmas tree decorations.

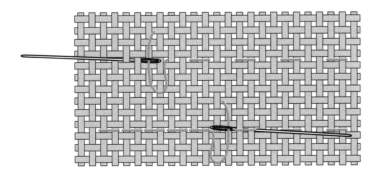

Starting and finishing with no knots

Knots at the back will appear as unsightly bumps on the front of your work when it is finally pressed and mounted. They will even pop right through the weave if it

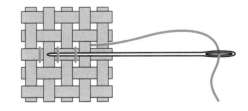

is loose enough. So, when starting out, push your needle through from the wrong side leaving a 3 cm [1.5 in] tail of thread at the back. Hold the tail against the fabric as you go and it will soon be caught down by the new stitches.

The correct way to fasten off is to run the thread under three or four wrong-side stitches, either horizontally or vertically. Whipping the end around one of those stitches helps to secure it.

THE HISTORY OF SAMPLERS

The word 'sampler' is derived from the French 'examplaire' meaning a model to be copied. Samplers were the forerunners of printed patterns, collections of stitches and motifs for sewing onto household linens and clothes. The earliest reference is recorded in 1502 on a bill of accounts for Elizabeth of York, wife of the English king Henry VII: 'for an elne of lynnyn cloth for a sampler for the Quene'. An ell measured 115 cm or 45 in.

Early English samplers were sewn on narrow linen strips, about 15–23 cm (6–9 in.) cut across the width of the loom on which they were woven. Cloth was very expensive and designs were worked into every spare fibre. They displayed a huge variety of stitches in as many as twenty different colours of silk and metal threads.

Germany produced the first printed pattern book in 1523 and by the end of the century so did every other European country. The oldest surviving sampler, was signed and dated by Jane Bostocke of England in 1598 and certainly shows the influence of such patterns.

During the next century it became fashionable to add a border of geometric or floral design and from about 1650 moral inscriptions were included. The idea of the sampler as an educational tool had arrived and it then became a record of virtue and achievement.

Throughout the 1700s, samplers changed to a square format and into highly ornamental pictures, maps, and even mathematical tables, all of which were intended to show off the needleworker's skill .

By the end of the nineteenth century and the close of the Victorian era, the craze for the needlework motto had taken over. Pre-printed on perforated paper and sold for pennies, it usually featured a domestic or rural scene and a proverb or quotation from the Bible. Cross stitch was the dominant stitch and schoolchildren and hobbyists everywhere could produce very satisfying results.

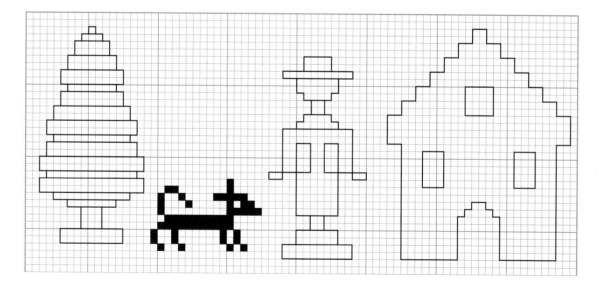

Four traditional sampler motifs: a tree, a dog a man and a house

ASSISI WORK

Thirteenth-century Italian embroidery consisting of a 'voided' (blank) motif, outlined in Holbein stitch (p. 133), surrounded by a background of solid or staggered cross stitch (p. 133).

Formal subjects suit Assisi work, like heraldic beasts or wild creatures, traditionally arranged in symmetrical pairs between intricate borders (p. 140) worked in the same colour as the background. Here are an eagle, a stag, a seahorse and a lion, all adaptable for Assisi-style projects.

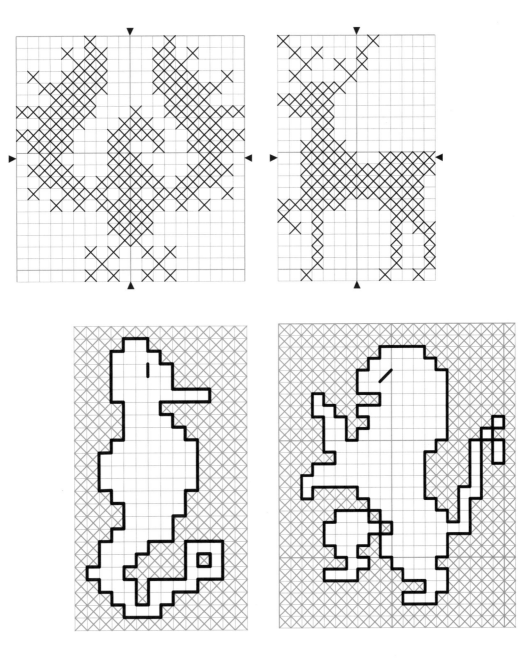

PART THREE

STITCHABLES AND FINISHING TOUCHES

GREETINGS CARDS

Special occasions deserve to be marked with cards that people will treasure. Even for regular events like birthdays and New Year, hand-embroidered greetings send a special message.

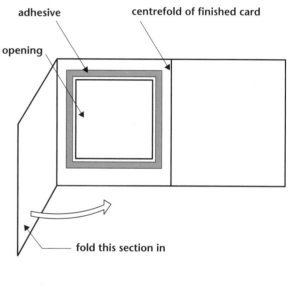

adhesive

centrefold of finished card

opening

fold this section in

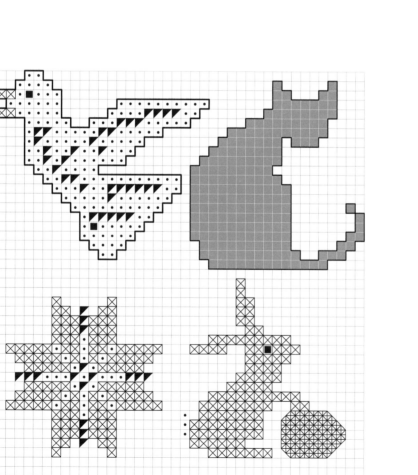

SERIF ALPHABET PLUS NUMERALS

Turn to page 36 for the Backstitch Alphabet and its matching numerals. It has the flavour of
a traditional sampler and looks good using only two strands of embroidery thread [floss].

BORDERS AND CORNERS

An essential feature of samplers and Assisi work, borders are worked once the main design is complete. Clever use of colour can create a three-dimensional effect. Only one or two strands of thread are required for a fine-line backstitch border.

DECORATIVE HEMS

Table runners, table cloths, napkins and other items need hemming once the embroidery is done.

Mitring

Mitring the corners enables them to lie flat with the rest of the hem.

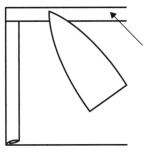

1 Press the raw edges to the wrong side (WS) right round the hem area. Fold under again by the same amount to make a double hem.

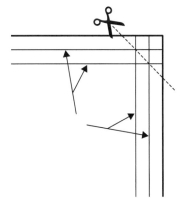

2 Unfold fabric to reveal four little squares creased into each corner. Trim each corner by cutting the inner square in half on the diagonal.

3 Fold each cut corner over, so the fold falls diagonally across the remaining creases.

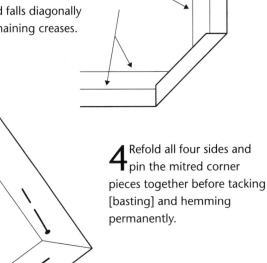

4 Refold all four sides and pin the mitred corner pieces together before tacking [basting] and hemming permanently.

Hemming

Most pieces of work are finished with a plain hem folded towards the wrong side of the material but you could try turning it to the right side instead, as in C, and – once you have done the initial slip hemming with ordinary thread – add some decorative stitching.

Alternatively, finish the normal hem with scallop stitches, as in A and B, or overcast as in D. These stitches can be organized in countless ways and colours.

For hems with scallop stitching, as with A and B, start embroidering from the left with vertical stitches, keeping the thread looped under the needle.

Where the stitches are angled, as with C, it is necessary to pass the needle through the folded fabric right out to the edge.

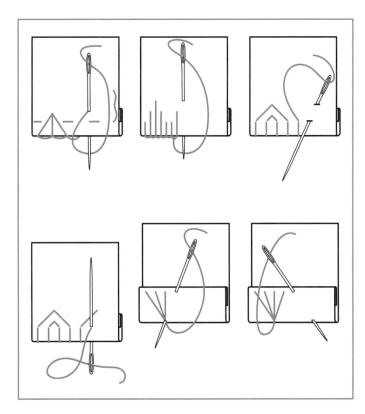

MOUSE PIN CUSHION

This cross-stitched mouse will keep your pins safe. You can even hook him up or pin him down by his tail.

YOU WILL NEED

14-count Aida fabric 25 x 15 cm [10 x 6 in] for the body (a higher count means smaller stitches)

Scraps of felt for the ears

Stranded embroidery cotton [floss] in three shades, plus or including black

Filling

Work the cross stitch with two or three strands of embroidery cotton on the Aida fabric before cutting it out. Use an embroidery hoop if you wish.

First, trace or copy two paper patterns of the mouse side, which includes a 6 mm [1/4 in] seam allowance. Cut out the paper shapes and pin them to the Aida as mirror images. Trace around them with a fabric marker. Mark and cut the ear slits C-D, you will work the cross stitch threads over the raw edges at those points.

Well-known to patchworkers as Tumbling Blocks, this pattern is worked in three colours – one light, one mid-tone and one dark, for best effect. You can embroider into the seam allowance but don't go beyond the cutting line.

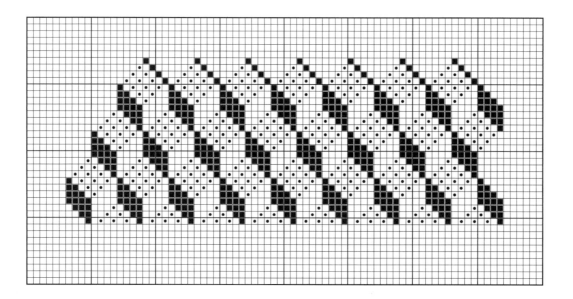

If you prefer to decorate the side of your mouse with somebody's initials or a single motif (see pp. 36, 137 and 142), chart your own stitch pattern, and begin stitching in the centre of each side, so the motif is well-positioned.

LENGTH: 10 cm [4 in]   LEVEL: BEGINNER

When cross stitch is done, cut out all pattern pieces.

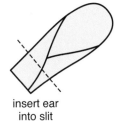

insert ear
into slit

1 Fold ears in on themselves and insert into the slits (C-D) on each of the body sides.

2 Thread a needle with two strands of black embroidery floss. Knot the end of the thread.

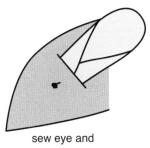

sew eye and
secure ear

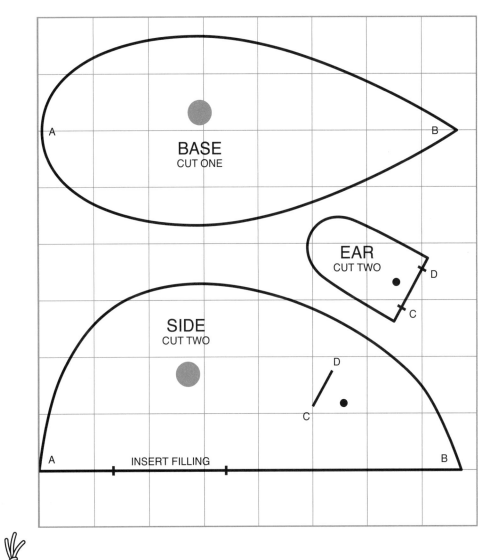

BASE
CUT ONE

A   B

EAR
CUT TWO

D

C

SIDE
CUT TWO

D

C

A   INSERT FILLING   B

3 Needle through from the wrong side (WS), stitch once or twice through body and ear. Bring needle out on the right side (RS) and make a French knot (p. 21) to create the eye.

4 Repeat for the other side.

5 Cut three 20 cm [8 in] strands of embroidery thread for the tail. Tie a knot in one end and plait as far as you wish before tying off with a knot and leaving a small tassel end.

6 Place body sides RS (with ears) together and stitch the spine from B to A.

7 Insert base section and sew up one side completely from nose (B) to tail (A).

8 Insert the tail centrally on the back seam with only the base knot sticking out. The rest of the tail should be inside the mouse for now.

9 Sew up the other side, leaving a gap for turning and filling.

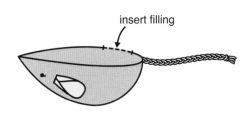

insert filling

10 Turn in the remaining raw edges and close gap neatly with slip stitch.

MINIATURE DESIGNS

There are many readymade items available from needlecraft suppliers. Small objects like key fobs, brooches, coasters, lids for pots and little boxes are an encouraging way of starting – and finishing – a cross stitch project. As gifts they can be given the personal touch of initials or designed to match a particular colour scheme. Other mini projects, such as coin purses, travel card wallets, scissor keepers and pin cushions are a good way of utilising your own stash of scrap fabrics and threads. Miniatures stitched from the patterns below will require fabrics of 14-count and upwards (remembering the higher the thread count, the smaller the stitch).

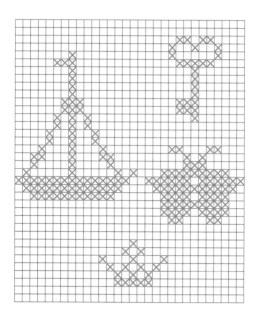

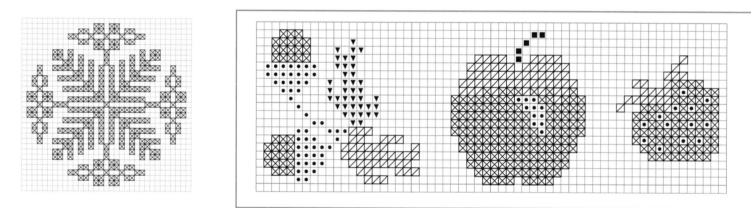

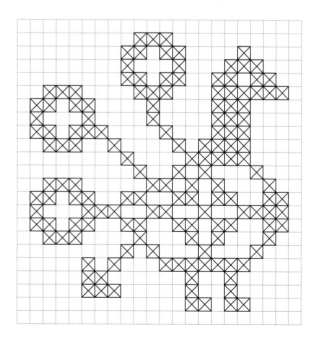

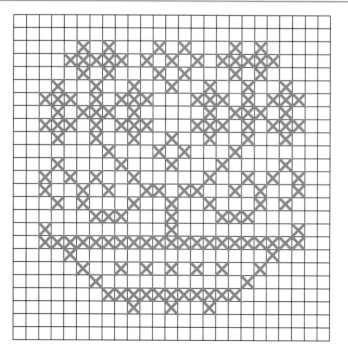

GLOSSARY OF CROSS STITCH TERMS

Aida   block weave fabric with regular construction and visible stitch holes

Alphabets   charted letters and numerals for samplers and monograms

Assisi   thirteenth-century embroidery technique from the Italian town of the same name

Away waste knot   starting knot placed well away from the stitching area and later cut off

Backstitch   used to outline or define cross-stitched areas

Band   narrow strip of evenweave fabric with decorative trim

Batting (wadding)   material used to pad mounted fabric

Binca   low-count (large scale) aida for use by children

Blackwork   decorative stitching, originally in black silk

Blending filament   fine metallic thread for combination with ordinary stranded cotton [floss]

Blocking   stretching and pinning fabric to shape

Bodkin   large blunt-tipped needle for threading ribbon and cord

Border   decorative frame stitched around a design

Chart   detailed guide to stitch placement in counted-thread embroidery, usually in the form of a grid or graph

Count   number of threads per 2.5 cm [1 in] in a foundation fabric

Counted-thread embroidery   technique of decorative stitching over a predetermined number of threads in the foundation fabric

Double running (Holbein) stitch   used in blackwork and Assisi work, constructed from two passes of running stitch

Duo canvas   canvas with a double thread mesh, also called Penelope

Embroidery canvas   starched woven cotton or linen mesh in four count sizes

Embroidery frame   rectangular frame to keep embroidery taut while working

Embroidery hoop   frame of concentric hoops to keep embroidery taut

Evenweave   fabric constructed with single threads of identical thickness crossing each other at right angles

Flower thread   unmercerised cotton twist, non-divisible, with a matt finish

Fractional stitches   quarter-, half- and three-quarter cross stitches

Fray stopper   liquid or spray to prevent fraying of cut edges

French knot   embroidery stitch used for small details

Grid   basis of a chart or pattern, each square representing one stitch

HPI   holes per inch

Holbein (double running) stitch   used in blackwork and Assisi work, constructed from two passes of running stitch

Key   list of symbols and associated colours on stitch charts

Laying tool   small pointed stick of metal or wood for smoothing threads

Making up   stretching and mounting finished work

Metallics   threads incorporating metal and textile fibres

Motif   one single design element

Open filling stitch   cross stitch variation

Penelope canvas   canvas with a double thread mesh, also called duo

Perforated paper   thin card perforated with holes in a grid formation in imitation

of Victorian-style stitched cards and
mottos.

Perle (pearl) shiny 2-ply twisted thread,
non-divisible

Plastic canvas plastic perforated to form
a rigid mesh

RS right side

Sampler decorative means of displaying
a variety of embroidery stitches

Skein length of embroidery cotton [floss]
held together by paper bands and colour
coded for reference

Space-dyed different colours or shades,
factory dyed at regular intervals along the
thread

Staggered cross stitch an alternative,
non-aligned version of cross stitch

Stranded cotton or rayon threads [floss]
consisting of divisible strands

Tacking [basting] preliminary stitching,
removed when work is finished

Tweeding different coloured strands
threaded into the same needle, used for
textural effect

Variegated factory-dyed single colour
ranging from light to dark at regular
intervals along the thread

Vilene non-woven interfacing, available
plain or iron-on

Wadding [batting] material used to pad
mounted fabric

WS wrong side

Waste knot starting knot placed on RS of
fabric and later cut off